To David & Dawn,
 Great being with you this weekend!
 May your journey be blessed!
 [signature]

Learning to Fly as a Nightingale

A Motivational Love Story

by
Diana Nightingale

The Keys Company Inc.

Copyright ©1989 by Diana Nightingale
All rights reserved. No part of this work covered by the copyright herein may be reproduced or used in any form or by any means — graphic, electronic, or mechanical, including photocopying, recording, taping or information storage and retrieval systems — without the written permission of the publisher.

First Edition published 1997
Keys Co., Inc.
Unlocking Doors through Education™

Library of Congress Catalog Card: 96-095321

ISBN: 0-9655760-0-0

Designed and Typeset by PhoeniX Productions, Inc.; Chicago, IL
Printed by Dynamic Graphix, Inc.; Clearwater, FL

Printed in the United States of America

Dedication

*"Never say never,
Our mother replied,
Better to say in all things that,
I tried.
Know I am with you though we are apart,
Live life with a song,
and God in your heart."*

                              For Mother,
                            In loving memory.

nightingale, *'the night singer'*. A migratory bird, genus Luscinia, belonging to the thrush family, esp. the European species, well known for the sweet singing of the male at night.

Foreword

This is a book of many facets. The magical journey of two inspiring life explorers, Diana and Earl Nightingale. I have had the privilege of knowing them both.

The canvas Diana weaves gives hope and a deep connectedness that we all share in this human experience.

You will share a bond with Diana as she unfolds their incredible love story. Two kindred spirits sharing the mystery and magic of male, female relationship.

In all our lives there are great joys and sorrows. This is true as night follows day. I feel Diana has felt these both deeply.

As Earl inspired millions daily with his five minute radio program, you will feel inspired by this book to work towards richer relationships.

Tova Borgnine

Introduction

Learning to Fly as a Nightingale began as a nocturnal fledgling, shortly after Earl's death; when moments and memories came flooding back, so clear, so painful, that the only way to deal with them was to write them down and tuck them away.

Thinking back on my marriage to Earl, I saw that it had been many things. Of course, it meant being supportive of his career; but that had been simple. Even before we met, we shared the same belief system and philosophies. So working together was a real joy.

Our marriage included all the challenges that face most couples, such as health problems, financial crisis and stepchildren issues. Life hadn't been any easier for us than anyone else. We had taken risks that didn't always turn out well, always assumed responsibility for our actions. And when we made a wrong choice, cut our losses and began again. We made every effort to be in charge of our lives.

People used to tell us they thought we were unique — although we never believed that. Earl used to say, "Honey, we're problem solvers. That's the only difference between us and most people. We find solutions."

We had our share of bad days, tough times, times of doubt and times of fear — just like everyone else. We simply chose to face life with a more positive attitude than most people. In addition to attitude, we both worked very hard at everything we did, believing that all the answers and everything we needed in life was out there, somewhere. We just kept searching until we found the answers we were looking for.

Introduction

We seldom gave up. We kept on trying, kept on believing, always expecting the best.

Being Mrs. Earl Nightingale required me to do and be many things in the public eye; but the richest part of the experience was very personal. Each of us had searched a very long time, always believing that our someone special was out there somewhere looking for us. Our marriage was a grand celebration of a man and a woman who had spent so many years apart, dreaming and searching for the perfect relationship. We found all that we were looking for in each other.

Hundreds of thousands of people around the world mourned Earl's death. There was a great outpouring of messages of condolences sent to me when Earl died. In the years since, many, knowing how difficult it was for me to go on without him, have asked for help in coping with the loss of their loved ones.

For millions of people around the world, Earl Nightingale is a Legend. Because of Earl's radio program, *Our Changing World*, his audio programs and his books, countless numbers of lives have been enhanced. For many of you, Earl Nightingale continues to live through the books he wrote or the sound of his voice on audio programs.

Through the years, I have received wonderful letters from many of you — people I have never met — sharing your stories about your lives or asking for guidance with your burdens. It's out of the affection for each of you that I introduce you now to Earl Nightingale, the man.

In so doing, you will get to know the Legend. Perhaps you will discover his work for the first time, and find your life enhanced, as have so many others.

People have always been, and continue to be, fascinated with our love story. And that is the story I share here — how we met, fell in love, or as Earl would say, "fell in love, then met" — and some of our adventures during our brief, but beautiful journey together. I have added nothing to our real life experiences and have tried to be as accurate as memory will allow.

Writing this book was, first and foremost, a great gift to myself. Long hours were spent remembering times in my life of great happiness — and great sorrow.

In reliving my life on paper, I now see how much I've grown; how much I've been strengthened. I've also discovered I was *Learning to Fly as a Nightingale*, even at times I thought I couldn't possibly go on.

Ultimately, the same beliefs and principles that governed our lives together, helped me go on alone after Earl left. True, they were easier to follow with him at my side; but holding fast to those beliefs has made life easier without him.

By sharing this abridged version of my life, I hope to help you see your life as a wonderful journey, a "holiday on earth", as Earl called it. May it encourage you to meet the challenges of life and go on in your darkest hours, when it seems you are most alone.

I hope you will discover, as I did, that this gift of life is precious in itself. People are given to or taken away from our lives not as reward or punishment, but as temporary gifts. I have learned that's the way life is.

I've also learned that death is the other side of birth. And the span of life in between should be lived at the highest possible level, whether we are sharing it with someone or not.

I would be very ungrateful, if I looked at my life and was disappointed that it didn't turn out just the way I wanted. It is, after all, a gift; special, unique and meant for me alone and given to me by our Creator.

Not one day passed that Earl and I didn't express our appreciation for the time and the love we'd been given. It was the power of that love that enabled us to go on to our next destinations separately. We lived our time together to the fullest.

Introduction

And, when it was time to part, Earl left this world with his hopes and dreams fulfilled. He took my love with him. Our love knows no boundaries.

Learning to Fly as a Nightingale is like our life together — not long, but wide and deep; and made of the stuff that dreams are made of.

"What kind of book is it?" someone asked recently. I thought about it for a minute, and decided that — as close as I can tell — it's a motivational love story.

Acknowledgements

After Earl died, I was grounded with a broken wing. During that time, and for eight years afterward, I wrote *Learning to Fly as a Nightingale*. To those special, loving people who were there to care, comfort and encourage me during that period, I give my deepest love and gratitude.

To my children/best friends Kim Bloomberg, Dayne Johnson, Jill and Jerome Fressinier; my grandchildren Dan, Sabra, Jordan and Juliette, you were truly the wind beneath my wings!

To my sisters Mary, Dorothy and Vanny and my brother John and their spouses, whose love for me never fails.

To Tova Borgnine, who called me twice a day, no matter where she was in the world. To Toni Boyle who had walked the road before me and lovingly guided my steps along the way. To Linda Simpson, MaryEllen Stanton and Joan Levenson, who saw me with my feathers ruffled and loved me still.

To Bob Atwood, who provided me with the ideal environment in which to write.

To Pat Arnold, who came into my life as a special friend/sister in spirit; then endeared herself to me for life when she saved my "tale" by editing my manuscript and preparing it for publication.

Most of all, to our heavenly Father, who authors my life and blesses me with such wonderful people!

Preface

There's an old fable about a prairie chicken who finds an abandoned eagle egg. Day after day, the chicken sits dutifully on the egg, keeping her vigil.

At last, the fledgling hatched. And the chicken cared for him as her own; teaching him all the ways of prairie chickens.

The young eagle spends his days scratching away in the dust and dirt for something to eat.

One day, while scratching about, he notices a shadow on the ground, and looks up into the sky. There, among the clouds and a backdrop of blue, was a great, magnificent bird.

"What is that, Mother?" he asks.

"Oh, that's an eagle," she replies. "They are the most powerful of all birds. They can fly very high and see for long distances, floating along with the clouds. They can hunt for food on land or fish in the seas."

"I'd like to be an eagle and fly like that," the fledgling said wistfully.

"Well, we're just prairie chickens. We can't fly," his mother responded.

The fledgling watched the eagle for a very long time, wishing with all his heart he could be up there, soaring high on the wind currents. He watched and watched until at last, the eagle flew out of sight. Then, with a heavy heart, the fledgling went back to scratching about in the dust, spending the rest of his days acting like a prairie chicken — never knowing that he, too, was an eagle.

Chapter 1

The Balloon Man standing by the roadside
selling childhood dreams
in blue and green and yellow, tied.
Floating, dancing, shiny red --
Holding all of a woman's future
hopes and dreams by a slender thread.
                              Diana Nightingale

In the late 1940s, people led quiet lives. Television hadn't come to the average home; so, entertainment sometimes required a vivid imagination. In the evenings, Americans huddled around their radios, listening to variety shows, serials and comedies; creating the sets and designing the costumes in their minds.

Life was pretty routine. At our house, we typically went to church on Sundays, came home, had dinner; then listened to our favorite radio programs. When the weather permitted, we spent quiet afternoons and evenings taking walks and sitting on the porch.

The best Sundays I can remember were when my mother, father and I drove to Elyria to visit my married sisters and my nieces, Jackie and Judy, who were just a couple of years younger than I. The 23 miles seemed endless, as I sat in the back seat of our black Pontiac 8 Silver Streak watching for the landmarks indicating we were getting closer: the old brown cow that grazed in the field at the corner where we turned. But my favorite landmark was the balloon man.

We usually left early, during the busiest part of the day. Our route took us past the Cleveland Hopkins Airport, just beneath the flight path.

Cars always were parked along both sides of the highway as people watched airplanes land and take off. For many of them, that would be as close as they would ever get to an airplane.

For me, the trip past the airport held a special kind of excitement. As we'd get closer, I'd sit as tall as I could; straining my eyes to see the rainbow of color that would let me know that *he* was there. My heart raced with excitement, as we drew closer and the colors came in sight.

There, in all his glory, stood the old man with his huge display of colorful balloons and monkeys on sticks. Unable to hold back any longer, excitedly I'd cry, "Daddy, Daddy, can I please have a balloon?"

My father would smile and say, "Yes, of course. But I'll tell you what — if I turn the car around, now to get to the other side of the street, I might cause an accident. And you wouldn't want that now, would you? And if we got a balloon, it would just get broken today. So, if he's there on the way back, I'll stop and get one for you then."

I would be so happy with the promise of my balloon and the anticipation that later, when it was time to leave, the idea of my balloon more than compensated for the sadness of parting with my playmates. But each time we'd approach the airport, the balloon man would be gone. My little heart would drop to the pit of my stomach, overwhelmed by my disappointment.

"Next time," my father would say. But each week, each visit, it would be the same. Daddy would promise and I'd believe him. And when we'd head home, the balloon man would be gone. Eventually, I stopped asking. And as we drove by, I'd press my face and hands to the window and sadly swallow the beautiful balloons with my eyes.

For many years, I carried that pain with me; never forgetting that my father had not once stopped to buy me a balloon. How sad, I thought. He didn't realize how little it would have taken for me to have happy tokens of the trips.

Instead, I had painful memories that my father had delighted in outsmarting his little girl.

When I was grown and had children of my own, I continuously tried to fill my own need for a balloon by buying my kids more balloons and monkeys on sticks than they ever wanted.

Many years later, I was living in Florida and my father came to visit.

He was in his eighties and in poor health. But he said he didn't want to just sit around and do nothing. He wanted to see the local attractions.

Since he always had enjoyed flowers and gardening, I suggested a tour of the Thomas Edison home and museum. My father thought that sounded like fun, so we jumped in the car and headed for town.

When we arrived, the tour had just left. So we decided to kill time in the gift shop. Dad wanted to buy some post cards for his friends back home. I headed in the other direction to browse. After some time had passed, someone came up behind me and touched me on the arm. I spun around. It was Dad. He handed me a small, flat package wrapped in brown paper.

"This is for you," he said.

"What is it?" I asked.

Tears welled in his eyes.

Seeing my father teary-eyed unnerved me. I stood, staring at him. He was old, but handsome; his rugged Greek features, accented by his newly-acquired suntan. His thick silver hair crowned his good-looking face.

"Just a little plate to hang on your kitchen wall," he said. "Remember when you were a little girl and wanted a balloon all those times? I have something to tell you. I knew the balloon man would be gone when we came back. I'm sorry I never bought you a balloon. And I hope you'll remember that whenever you look at this plate."

We stood there, Dad holding one side of the little package; I, the other, as my tears began to flow.

It was the first and only time I can remember my father holding me when I cried.

Chapter 2

*My mother cried;
but then there was a star danced,
and under that I was born.*
                    William Shakespeare (1599)

There will always be moments, like the one I shared with my father, that are frozen in time and space. Isolated incidents that may seem ordinary at the time – all those rides past the balloon man – but are cornerstones for building our belief systems for the rest of our lives.

For most of us, the most influential moments seem to occur when we are young, when we have no history of our own from which to draw our comparisons. We take what happens to us or is told to us by adults as the final truth – like being told we're prairie chickens, when we're actually eagles.

For many of us, childhood dreams include plans for the future; a time when we would be grown and independent. As a fledgling still in the nest, I dreamed of the day my wings would be strong enough that I could leave and begin my search, my journey, to know who I was and where I belonged.

Without having to be told, some information just seemed to be a part of me – like knowing with all my heart that there was God. I just knew Him, and knew He was with me.

As a child, I can remember spending hours lying in the grass, staring into the sky and thinking about all kinds of things; thinking maybe there was something different about me, that I wasn't really like the other kids; dreaming about growing up and having children of my own.

Besides lying in the grass, I did other important things like riding my bike, roller skating, playing with my dolls, eating chocolate ice cream, playing baseball and helping my friend Sue sabotage Bobby Sharp's yard.

One Sunday evening when I was about eight or nine years old, my mother, father and I were driving through Lorain, Ohio. As usual, I was riding in the back seat of our family car. The moment is so vivid, it could have happened yesterday. I can still feel the rough material of the seat as I sat there looking out the window.

At that time, Lorain was a dirty, smelly, steel mill town, dark with pollution. The heat and humidity were so intense, we had the windows of the car open. Trying to catch a breeze, families were gathered outdoors on porches and on steps, laughing, talking, while children my age played ball and jumped rope in the streets.

For some reason, I became uncomfortable and wanted to distance myself from the scene outside. I reached over and locked my car door. I wasn't afraid that someone was going to get in the car, *I just wanted to shut out that world.*

In my imagination, I had been born in Lorain. I was one of the children on these dirty streets. I imagined that my parents would move away from this place and take me somewhere else. If they didn't, I thought I'd have to leave home as soon as I was able.

As we drove through the city, I wondered where I'd live when I grew up. I knew I would move on, and would keep on going until I had found the place where I belonged.

That probably was the first goal I'd ever set. But of course I was too young to know anything about goals. Most of the adults of that time didn't either. They just believed what they were told about who and what they were, letting life happen to them, not unlike the misinformed eagle/prairie chicken.

I always thought my mother would have loved that story and certainly could have identified with that prairie chicken.

She, like so many women of her generation, was expected to give up her dreams; to live as something or someone else, according to what her family and society expected.

Mother was a beautiful woman, from the time she was very young until the day she died. In addition to her beauty, she had a marvelous sense of humor and was blessed with a beautiful singing voice.

While still in her teens, she drew the attention of Madam Bartlett, a voice teacher from England who had come to Elyria to visit friends. Madam Bartlett and a friend were taking a walk; and through an open window, heard Mother singing and playing the piano.

She was so impressed with the quality of Mother's voice that she offered to take her back to England, to coach Mother and prepare her for a career in music.

For Mother, it was a dream come true; and she desperately wanted to go. But my grandmother wouldn't hear of such a thing. No self-respecting young woman would go off on such a "wild goose chase". Mother, who was only seventeen, could not go without Grandma's permission.

Her dreams smashed, Mother was destined to remain at home like all the other "prairie chickens" instead of soaring with the eagles.

One day, the small town was buzzing with news. Four handsome young Greeks from Samos Island were looking for places to rent.

Grandma and Grandpa had a big house and rented out rooms from time to time. Hearing about Grandma's home, one of them came to ask about lodging. While he was talking with Grandma, Mother came down the stairs. The young man told me many years later that when he looked up, he saw the most beautiful woman he had ever seen. He said she looked like an angel.

Grandma saw this man as the future she had in mind for her daughter; certainly preferable to a music career in England. With a great deal of intercession from Grandma, the two were soon married.

Mother's musical fantasies took her as far as the dime store in downtown Elyria, where she played piano and sang the lyrics of the sheet music sold in the store. She simply closed her eyes and pretend she was somewhere else.

Mother did what was expected of women of her time. She married and raised a family. At eighteen she had her first baby girl, Mary, followed by a second and third daughter before presenting her Greek husband his son, John. Duty accomplished, she took a deep breath. Eleven years later, just when she saw the light at the end of the birth canal, I appeared.

While loving us dearly and dedicating herself to us completely, Mother hated the experience, because she had not chosen it.

But we had no way of knowing. She was a great, great mom! But, if she had followed her heart or had been born at a later time, I'm sure she would have chosen a different path.

She never stopped singing. We always had a piano at home. And every evening after cleaning the kitchen, Mother and I would sit at our old upright. She played and we'd sing. She showed me the covers of the sheet music, with the pictures of the movie stars who made the songs famous. When the movies came to our local theater, we'd go and see all the musicals. Those were happy times for both of us. Sometimes, when the rest of the family came home, we'd put a family band together, singing and laughing for hours. I have always been glad that Mother taught me to sing. She, no doubt, was preparing me for my life as a Nightingale.

Mother's music liberated her mentally, as she fulfilled her obligations as mother and wife. Once we were on our own, though, you couldn't catch her. She took bus trips from coast to coast and moved from Ohio to Florida and back, as the mood hit her. As I grew older, I learned to appreciate all that Mother had sacrificed for us. I admired her for doing such a good job and teaching us so much, meeting challenges and recognizing the rewards of duty.

Mother never allowed us to say, "I can't," and discouraged us from ever quitting. She insisted that we always begin our task with, "I'll try." Then, to give us an extra hand, she taught us that God was with us always and with Him, all things were possible. She'd smile and say, "You can do it – try."

Mother also taught me that being a female should not preclude me from trying whatever I desired. She said life wasn't intended to be gender-programmed. So, when I was little, we'd listen to boxing on the radio with the same enthusiasm as we did *Fibber Magee and Molly*, *The Shadow* and *Sky King*.

In later years, the TV would be telecasting car racing, while Mother taught me to lay out patterns and sew on her old Singer machine.

Music of all kinds always played when we were cooking, baking or gardening. Everything we did, we did to music.

Mother was as fastidious in her appearance and dress as she was beautiful. She tried to instill in me her values about personal appearance.

She was well-disciplined in her grooming habits and used to tell me that a woman should always be sure to, "Get up, bathe, dress and put on your make-up. If someone drops by unexpectedly, you will be forgiven for dishes in the sink, left over from breakfast. But if you look bad, you'll never hear the end of it."

It was a ritual for us to wear hats and gloves whenever we went shopping in downtown Cleveland. Always a lady, Mother neither smoked nor drank.

But life wasn't all song and fantasy for me as a child. Mom and Dad's marriage was bad, perhaps from the start. Finally, after 34 years of marriage and five children, they decided to divorce. I was a freshman in high school at the time. Mother was concerned about the trauma that this might cause me at this vulnerable time of my life. She wanted to find a way to provide a good, strong influence through my high school years.

My two best friends, Carol and Judy, and I were inseparable the summer following the divorce. Judy's dad was a policeman and, next to mine, her mother was the best in town. Judy had several brothers; and her house was everyone's second home. It was a good, safe place to be.

Mother liked my friends and their families. So when school started in the fall, even though we were not Catholic, she decided I should transfer to the parochial school Carol and Judy attended. She thought it would offer me the support of my friends, as I transitioned to a single-parent home.

I didn't care one way or the other. I was popular at my old school. But I liked the idea of being with Judy and Carol on a daily basis and sharing school activities with them.

So, I enrolled in the parochial school my sophomore year. I was spotlighted as the school's only Protestant – a potential convert. So the nuns and priest went out of their way to make me welcome. I was in chorus, drama and became captain of the cheerleaders. I was an average student, but I was well-liked and well-known.

Perhaps because I wasn't Catholic, I always had felt a close relationship with God and His Son, Jesus Christ. But, as I grew older I wanted to know more about Them. And I wondered how best to worship them. Attending Catholic school, I thought, offered a great opportunity for me to find out.

I had tons of questions, endless questions. Father John used to blush when he ran out of answers for me. Sister Genevieve used to say, "Just have faith and you won't need answers."

One evening, we were preparing for a special religious event; so choir practice was held in the church loft. As we were leaving, Sister stopped us at the bottom of the loft steps. She told us to be sure and stop at the altar on the way out and pay homage to an old relic from some long-deceased pope.

I was standing on the bottom step, while other choir members bunched-up behind me. I asked for details.

Who was this? What was this relic thing? What did she want us to do, I wanted to know. Sister drew me aside, while several of my friends followed behind. She explained that this pope was very special; and that a tiny piece of his robe was encased in plastic. We were to kneel and kiss it out of respect and love.

"I can't do that," I said.

Sister's eyes got really big. "What do you mean, you can't do that?"

"It's not right, Sister. That's idolatry. And Sister, about the statues – that bothers me too. It's against God's commandment."

Father John had joined us by now. You would have thought that I had pulled the pin out of a hand grenade and threatened the lives of the entire student body. Two nuns grabbed me by the arms, and escorted me from the church, onto the front steps. They were furious!

One of them called me a troublemaker. She told me not to come to school the next day; that they didn't want people like me there.

The next morning, Mother and I received threatening phone calls. I was not welcome at Saint John Cantius any longer. I was a senior with two months until graduation. But, all of my records were removed, all pictures of me were omitted from our yearbook and I was unable to graduate with my class.

That is when I first realized that defending what I believed is costly. But the die had been cast. My first dues had been paid. Life would not be an easy assignment. But, Mother had raised me with options. I knew I would have her support, no matter what I chose to do with my life.

After school, I wanted to marry, have babies, and lead a quiet life. Two months before my eighteenth birthday, I married my Catholic high school sweetheart, converted to Catholicism and settled into what I thought would be "happily ever after." Four years later, the fairy tale ended.

My husband had never been faithful. He hung out with his buddies and had continued to date. On a VFW Drum and Bugle Corps trip with his mother and father, he met and became involved with a young woman from New York.

Her father allegedly was connected to the mob. He made my husband an offer he couldn't refuse, bought us an annulment and arranged for his daughter's marriage in St. Peter's Cathedral.

The only trace left of the marriage was our small daughter, Kim. Deeply disillusioned, I decided I could not find religious perfection in the Catholic Church. I explored other spiritual paths.

By the time I was 25, I had remarried and had achieved my first goal: I had three darling children. Life was good and I was happy. But something else was happening.

While I was busy being wife, mother and homemaker, my mind was racing – I mean all the time, racing — about the state of America. The girl who had been booted out of the Catholic school was still alive and well — and causing all kinds of problems with my friends and family. I seemed to have feelings, thoughts and opinions that were in conflict with most of theirs. It became obvious that I was indeed a strange bird.

For example, the civil rights movement was under way by now. I longed to join the marches in Selma and Washington. I was appalled and just couldn't believe that any American could be treated unjustly simply because of skin color or gender. That was not what I had been taught by my parents and the school system. What about the Constitution and the Bill of Rights? Hadn't we been taught that Lincoln freed the slaves and that men died in wars to preserve America's freedom? I believed we were all free and lived in unity under a blanket of democracy. Was I crazy or what?

Many others were thinking and feeling the same as I. They happened not to be in my immediate circle. That was a problem.

The same was true with my views on the Vietnam War. I didn't understand America's continued involvement. I didn't feel our soldiers should have been there so long and was upset with the way things were being handled.

Late one night, during the Cuban crisis, I was in the rocking chair nursing my son, Dayne. I looked down at my beautiful little baby boy and wondered how many other mothers were caring for their sons at this very same moment; all of us changing diapers and making sure our babies were fed, dry and warm. For what? So that after we raised them, educated them, loved them and protected them, we could send them off to kill and be killed at the command of their government?

"It's been that way since the beginning of time," I was told. That's a pretty stupid reason, I thought.

The body count rose in Vietnam; while we sat at home comfortably watching the war on TV, eating hamburgers and pizza. One night I got up, turned off the TV and said, "*Enough!* Our children will not grow up watching war and death and perceiving it as normal and acceptable."

Friends would tease me, saying that when the Russians invade the United States, I would be part of the welcoming party. I flippantly responded that I'd make spaghetti and we could solve our problems over dinner and a glass of Chianti. After all, they'd just be a bunch of young boys, far away from home for the first time; lonely, homesick and hungry.

Another friend, a college professor, loved engaging me in discussions about religion and God. He said if we had been born centuries earlier, everyone could pack picnic lunches, go down to the coliseum and watch Diana get thrown to the lions.

It was pretty clear to me, as well as to my contemporaries, that I did not belong to their flock; the same assessment I'd made when I was a child. I got no sympathy from Mother, either. She would say, "Count your blessings. You can't have it all."

I wondered if she was talking about her life or mine.

Then I'd wonder: How much is all? How far is too far? What is too fast, too high, too much?

My answer came later, as I watched young athletes receiving gold medals in the Olympics. They too wanted to test the limits and know what was "too far, too high, too fast". These people were called "winners". And they had a multitude of blessings to count, in addition to the gold medals recognizing their accomplishments. I, too, wanted to test my limits.

I was 42 when Earl Nightingale stepped onto my path. And when he appeared, he validated my entire being, my entire life. I was no longer a stranger in the world, an alien on a strange planet. I still wanted to test my limits. But for the first time, there was someone cheering me on; for the first time, I no longer was alone.

Earl used to say, our time on Earth is "our journey into meaning." None of us would begin a physical journey without a plan, a road map or a clearly defined destination. But we do it all the time when we embark upon a spiritual, or mental journey. Consequently, we often find ourselves somewhere lost in time and space, with nothing but thoughts, questions and feelings; none of which signals whether we're headed in the right direction.

We need to take time to mentally put things in order and decide whether its expedient to proceed without a plan. Do we take control of our future journey or let life just happen to us?

My journey into meaning was a solitary one for many years. Every once in a while, I would meet a "fellow traveler" and we would share the path for a time. More often than not, however, my companion would get distracted and fly off in another direction. It happened time and again. Until I encountered another rare bird.

Chapter 3

> *A bird of the air shall carry the voice,*
> *and that which hath wings shall tell the matter.*
> Ecclesiastes 10:20

Eighteen years before I was born, another fledgling was beginning his own flight, clear across the country in California.

Earl had been inquisitive from the time he was little in Long Beach, California. At twelve, he was obsessed with finding out why people turned out the way they did.

In particular, he wanted to know why his own family was so poor. They didn't have shoes and their food came from cans without labels. His mother, whom they called Honey, barely eked out an existence for herself and her three boys. The four of them were living in Tent City on the beach; the boys' dad having left for greener pastures some time before.

Honey and her neighbors said they, and everyone else, were poor because there was a Great Depression. That didn't make sense to Earl. He knew that wasn't true because just a few yards down the beach, people partied on yachts, tied up in the marina. Those people weren't poor – they were rich.

Earl asked everyone he met to explain the disparity to him. But no one was able to give him the answers he needed. His mom had taught him the value of reading, so he went to the public library in search of the answer. Earl read everything he could get his hands on from that day forward.

Throughout his childhood, Earl worked at anything and everything to make a dollar. One of his fondest memories was his job as a waffle cone maker on the pier.

He'd pour the batter into the waffle maker, then mold the waffles into ice cream cones. People would gather and watch, drawn there by the delicious smell of the cooking waffles drifting through the air.

As he got older, his desire to see the world and escape his meager surroundings, drove him and his old buddy, Matt, to hop freight trains up to San Francisco in the summer to find work.

One time, they arrived with only a few pennies between them. They were dirty, tired, and very hungry. They needed a plan in order to survive. They took the few pennies they had, bought some firecrackers and waited.

When they saw a policeman, they lit the firecrackers and set them off. As expected, the policeman arrested them and hauled them off to the police station where they put them to work for discharging the firecrackers in the city.

Earl and Matt had to shovel horse manure out of the stables and clean up the police station. But they also were able to eat, shower and had a clean, safe place to stay for a few nights – while they "learned their lesson"!

Another time, Earl hitched alone and cut his leg badly while jumping onto the train. A bad infection set in and he became unconscious. Another hobo on the train jumped off the train when it stopped and managed to get some medication for Earl's leg, then nursed the infection until they got to the city.

In his book, *Earl Nightingale's Greatest Discovery*, Earl wrote about his next years:

Later, as World War II loomed on the horizon, I left school and enlisted in the Marine Corps. But I continued my studies. I read everything I could lay my hands on. I made two decisions that guided the remainder of my life. The first was to discover the secret of success. The second was to become a writer. I loved books and wanted to write them myself.

Toward the end of the war, I found myself back in the States working as an instructor at Camp LeJeune, North Carolina.

Driving between the base and nearby Jacksonville, I noticed a radio station under construction.

I decided to apply for an announcing job, working nights and weekends. I auditioned and was hired. Sitting before the microphone at the small radio station, WJNC Jacksonville, North Carolina, was the beginning of my radio career.

I took to broadcasting like nothing before in my life. I was in my element, and it was to be part of my life for more than forty years.

But my desire to write did not lessen, and gradually I began planning for the day when I would write my own programs.

In the meantime, I learned the business; doing commercials, news, and station breaks. It was extra income and would prove to be invaluable experience after I was mustered out of the Marine Corps. My reading and search for the secret of success continued without letup. I studied the world's great religions. I found myself especially fascinated with philosophy and psychology.

But it wasn't until one weekend when I was twenty-nine and working for CBS in Chicago that enlightenment came. While reading, it suddenly dawned upon me that I had been reading the same truth over and over again for many years. I had read it in the New Testament, in the sayings of Buddha, in the writings of Lao Tse, in the works of Emerson.

And all of a sudden, there they were, the words, in the proper order that I had been looking for, for seventeen years. The astonishing truth that we become what we think about. It was as if I were suddenly immersed in a bright light. Of course! I remember sitting bolt upright at the thought of the simplicity of it.

That was what Ortega was talking about when he reminded us that we are the only creatures on earth born into a natural state of disorientation with our world. It had to be because we are the only creatures with the godlike power to create our own worlds. And we do.

And if we don't think at all – which seemed to have been the principal problem of the people back in my old Long Beach neighborhood – we don't become anything at all.

There it was, just six words. There are more than six hundred thousand words in the English language, but those were the six I had searched for, in that particular order, ever since the age of twelve. Seventeen years it had taken to see the obvious. How could we become anything else? Our minds are the steering mechanisms of our lives.

And each of us who does much thinking at all thinks differently.

There, at last, was the secret of success or failure or something in between.

Each of us is sentenced to become what he or she thinks about. Those six simple words, in that order, revolutionized my life. I had found them, clearly spelled out, just as I had so desperately hoped as a child of twelve to find them, not in some hoary, ancient tome, but in a book published in 1937 entitled <u>Think and Grow Rich</u> *by a man named Napoleon Hill.*

In 1956, Earl wrote a short essay based on his many years of reading and searching for the answer he found in *Think and Grow Rich.* He called his essay, *The Strangest Secret*. He had written it and recorded it, to be played in his absence to a small insurance sales staff.

In a short time, and without any real effort or marketing, its popularity grew. The men who'd heard it had told others about it and had requested copies for friends and relatives. No one had made a informational recording before. Therefore, there was much surprise when sales grew to over a million and he earned a Gold Record.

The demand was so great that Earl needed help distributing his work. His long-time friend, Lloyd Conant, was in the mail order business. He offered to help. Together, they formed the corporation that would be the seedling from which the entire informational recording industry would grow.

Earl's journey had, indeed, taken on meaning for him — and the people whose lives he touched. His radio, television, audio cassette and personal messages to audiences around the world revolved around his original essay and most highly recognized program, *The Strangest Secret*, which he defined in six words: "You become what you think about."

He also tried to impress upon his listeners that, in addition to becoming what we think about, it was and is vitally important to realize that the life given to us should be viewed as, "a holiday on Earth." Earl truly believed that the time between our creation and the next experience after life here on Earth is a precious holiday; our "journey into meaning."

I didn't know Earl in 1956 when he wrote *The Strangest Secret*. (I didn't even know until I met him years later that Mother and I had listened to him faithfully on the radio when he was the voice of *Sky King*.) It would be sixteen years before I even heard of Earl, and another ten before we met face-to-face.

But even before we met, we were soul mates. I, looking for that someone special in the world who would share my thoughts, hopes and dreams; while he was searching, he said, for the girl whose picture he carried in his mind and his heart.

Chapter 4

*And think not you can direct the course of love;
For love, if it finds you worthy,
directs your course.*
Kahlil Gibran

In 1972, I was living in Florida, divorced and raising my three children, working in real estate sales and being fed steady diets of mandatory motivational information by my employers. I hated the contrived concepts on how to manipulate someone to get what you wanted. I found little in the tapes and books that I personally could relate to and avoided them whenever I could.

One Friday afternoon, after an especially busy day, my broker asked me to come to his office. Phil had a set of tapes and a book entitled *This is Earl Nightingale.* He wanted me to read and listen to them. I wasn't interested; suspecting it was just more of the same old stuff. But Phil insisted that this was different and asked me to promise to check it out. He told me Nightingale was his hero and he just wanted to share his work with me.

I saw how important it seemed to him. So I promised I would give the material my full attention. I was eager to get my obligation over and began listening to the tapes that night after dinner. When I finished, I read the book.

It was very strange that, from the first tape to the end of the book, I felt a kindred spirit with the author. He instantly was a friend who spoke my language, read my mind and knew my heart. It made me feel good to know there was someone out there who thought and felt the way I did. I returned the book and tapes to the office Monday morning.

"Well? Did you listen – did you read? Were you impressed?" Phil obviously liked this Earl Nightingale a lot.

"Yes, I listened to all of the tapes and, yes, I read the book, too."

"Well, weren't you impressed?" he asked.

"Not actually," I said, matter-of-factly. "What I felt more than anything else was a great simpatico. His ideas and ideals are very much in tune with my own. I guess if I felt anything, it was the knowledge that if I were ever to meet this man, I would probably like him tremendously and we would have a great deal in common."

"That's great! Glad you loved him, too. I'm going to make you a gift of that book of his. Here, let me inscribe it to you."

About eight years later, still in Florida, still in real estate, I was working as a rental manager, booking tourists into local beach front hotels in the summer months. Because it was off-season, you could have fired a cannon through the lobbies of the hotel and not hit anyone. The sales staff was bored and found ways of passing the long, uneventful, days in ways that weren't always in keeping with company policy.

One hot, lazy afternoon, I was going over reservation bookings at one of the hotels when I noticed an elderly woman sitting alone in the reception area. She seemed to be waiting for someone and kept checking her watch. After some time had passed, I asked the receptionist if she knew if the woman had been helped or if she was a guest waiting for someone.

The receptionist's face flushed and she seem embarrassed. She said she didn't want to get anyone in trouble and made me promise not to tell anyone what the sales staff had done.

"It depends," I said. "What's going on?"

The sales staff was not supposed to leave the site at any time. There was a lunch room; but that day, the entire staff decided to go out to lunch – together. I don't know what caused this revolution. In addition, they had invited a psychic to come do readings for them.

The woman had called and said she was having car problems and couldn't come until later, so they left for lunch.

Apparently, the psychic solved her transportation problem and had arrived moments after they left. Now, this little elderly woman was sitting in an otherwise empty lobby.

If the owners dropped by, which they did on a regular basis, everyone would get fired. They were a great sales staff and I knew how bored they all were. They didn't usually do things like this.

During the busiest times, they were there early and went home late. They worked on scheduled days off if needed; and always without complaint. They were of good cheer, always making light of even the most stressful times.

I also knew, when they found out they'd gotten caught, they'd never do it again.

I crossed the lobby, introduced myself to the woman and asked if she wouldn't like to wait someplace more comfortable. She was pleasant. Her name was Margaret. And she said she'd like that very much.

We went up to one of the many empty apartments to wait for the sales staff. She was a delightful woman, the grandmotherly kind; *elderly* grandmother, that is. (Since I became a grandmother when I was 35, it's changed my perception of grandmothers.)

I brought her a cup of coffee and told her I expected the staff to return shortly. I assured her they would have privacy for their readings.

She thanked me, and said she could see much about my life. She asked if she could read for me while we waited. I remember feeling uncomfortable about it. But, in all honesty, I probably was more concerned that she would tell me how dismal my life would be in the future; that I had a long life of endless hard work and conflict ahead. But I said, "Oh sure, I'd love to hear what's in store for me."

She began by telling me a lot of accurate things about my kids and my life at the present. Then she said I was going to be changing jobs soon.

I remember chuckling to myself, "Yeah, right after I get caught having my palm read, I'll get fired!"

She said I was going to work for a very nice, honest man whose name was Mac something.

I confirmed that I was planning a job move. "But my new boss is a woman," I corrected her. "And her name isn't anything like Mac."

Completely disregarding my input, she went on to say that my life was going to change, drastically! It would take a complete about-face, and that the second half of my life was going to be as wonderful and eventful as the first half had been disappointing.

"Riiiight!" I thought.

She went on. There would be a man who would come from far away. We would meet, he would leave, I would follow him, we'd be married, and everything I had ever hoped for in life and in love would come true.

She also said the cruise I was planning would have to wait; but that it was okay because this man, my future husband, and I would take one that would be so wonderful I would be very glad I had waited for him to share it with.

Even though I didn't believe her predictions, I felt a lot happier about this fairy tale than if she had told me I would end up as a bag lady.

"Well, thank you," I said. "That was very nice. Now if you'll just wait here, the staff will be back soon."

"Some story," I thought. "The only thing she left out was – 'And they lived happily ever after.'"

Soon after my conversation with the psychic, the bank approved my mortgage loan; and I was able to make plans for my job and residential moves.

One evening, I was selecting wallpaper from a sample book when the phone rang. The caller asked if I remembered answering an ad some months earlier for a sales job.

I recalled responding to a vaguely-worded ad, recruiting personnel for timeshare sales. But, I no longer was interested, because I'd decided to accept another job.

We talked about my background and experience, and he asked if I would come to Punta Gorda for an interview. He felt, based on our conversation, that I was just the sort of person they wanted on their staff. I thanked him and told him I thought Punta Gorda was too far to travel. I was able to make good money closer to home without commuting in heavy traffic twice a day.

He asked me what I had to lose by just coming up for an interview and a tour of the apartments. I said I didn't think I could make it; but I'd see.

He said, "Saturday, two o'clock. Ask for Mr. White when you get here."

I thanked him, hung up and planned not to go.

When Saturday came, I had a busy morning running errands. I finished early, came home, fixed lunch and went in to take a shower. I thought, since I'd gotten everything done so early and didn't have anything else planned, maybe I'd drive up to Mr. White's Fisherman's Village in Punta Gorda, to check out the competition.

I finished my shower, got dressed and headed north. It was a pleasant drive and I was impressed with the Village when I arrived. I parked the car and walked into the reception area.

I asked the receptionist where I might find Mr. White. She started to explain something to me, changed her mind and gave me directions to an apartment upstairs. She told me the meeting was just starting.

I hurried. The apartment was crowded with applicants. As I walked into the apartment, a nice-looking man crossed the room and said, "You must be Diana."

I smiled and said, "Yes, I am. And you must be Mr. White."

Apparently everyone else had asked the same question because the room filled with laughter.

The man smiled back and said, "Actually, we use the names Mr. Black and Mr. White, so that we can tell where you heard about us and which ads are working for us. My name is Denny MacLaine. But you can call me Mac."

Mac! The psychic had said my new boss' name was Mac!

I quickly took my seat and paid close attention to everything that was being said. After all, if I was going to be working here, I'd want to know all I could about the place. The rest of my wonderful life was supposed to begin here.

December is usually a busy time of the year in the timeshare business. That year, it was especially busy for me and my younger daughter, Jill, as we hustled to paint and wallpaper our new condo. We finished, just in time to move in before Christmas.

It was hectic, trying to move plus having to go through the rigorous sales training at the Village. Besides that, their trainer didn't want women working on his team. He made life during training as challenging for me as he possibly could.

I had more pressing matters on my mind.

My mom was 84 years old and our time together was becoming more and more precious. Given my schedule, it was unlikely that I could visit her in Ohio. So, she came to Florida for a few weeks, amid the chaos of our move.

She was concerned about the way I lived my life and how I earned a living. I thought then, and still do, I was doing just fine. I owned a lovely condo, had a new car, a good income, and no debts.

Mother wanted me to have a "real job"; one where I got paid a salary instead of this unpredictable commission thing.

And why didn't I ever want to get married again, she wondered. That was unnatural. Every woman needed a man to take care of her, she insisted. Mom's ideas about women's roles seemed to have changed. She no longer thought women should pursue careers instead of relationships.

I'll never forget the look on her face when I said, "Look, Mom, you know I've tried marriage, more than once. It just doesn't work for me. I don't know how to look for 'Mr. Right' any more. And I've given up trying.

"I think I'm attracted to the wrong men for the wrong reasons. Only God knows what I need and whom I need.

"He's probably created someone special for me. I've either missed him or haven't met him, yet.

"I've prayed about it and I've made a deal with God. I promised Him that I won't look anymore. I'm just going to stand real still and let Him direct Mr. Right, so he can find me. He's probably been looking for me all of his life. And I've been so busy running around, he hasn't been able to find me.

"But one of these days when I least expect it, if God so wills, he'll walk up to me and say, 'I've been looking for you all of my life and knew you the minute I saw you.' God will direct us. I don't need to think about it or worry about it anymore."

She gave me that drop-dead look that only a mother could give. You know the one I mean.

"Well, next thing you'll tell me is that you expect him to knock at your door," she scolded. "You make it impossible to ever meet anyone with an attitude like that!"

I was sorry I was disappointing her. I knew how important it was to her that I be properly established as a wife. She had always worried about me being taken care of, if she wasn't around.

Mother was 42 when I was born. People of her generation just didn't live as long as we do now. I remember when I was small, she'd always say, "If the Good Lord will just let me live until you're out of grade school, I'll be thankful." She was worried then, as now, that I'd be left without her.

Being a child, I was sure that she was long overdue to die. I lived in constant fear that I'd come home from school one day and find her body.

Sometimes, when she was napping, I'd kneel down next to her to see if I could see her breathe. And if I wasn't sure, I'd softly touch her eyelashes to make her blink, so I'd know. If I woke her, I'd sheepishly say, "I just wanted to be sure you were still in there."

She would laugh and say, "I'm still here."

Years later, Mom couldn't believe the Good Lord had allowed her to live long enough to see me as a grandmother!

I laughed and reminded her that she didn't think she'd make it until I was out of grade school.

The Good Lord had let her live a long time and we were very close. Even though I'd had many years to prepare for her death, I still lived in dread that when she died, I wouldn't be able to bear the pain and survive without her.

Now here I was, a single grandmother and no plan to look for a man to share my "golden years." She must have thought she'd never see me in a secure relationship. She'd had to depend on herself after her divorce, especially in her golden years. In her mind, the only safe place for a woman was with a man.

I know how difficult it was for my mother to enter the workforce for the first time, in her mid-fifties. How lonely she must have felt at times. She didn't want me to suffer the same fate. I wasn't suffering at all.

Right after the new year, we were greeted by a big announcement at work: on Saturday, January 23, there would be an early sales meeting. Before I could groan, Mac assured me I would like it. Like it or not, he said, attendance was mandatory.

One of the partners in the development, Earl Nightingale, was scheduled to address the meeting. I, of course, was familiar with his work, since receiving his book years earlier. And a restaurant bearing his name was on the premises.

But I had no burning desire to get up extra early for a Saturday meeting. Why couldn't they have scheduled it one day after work, I wondered.

Mother was still visiting; and between wallpapering, going through the job training course, holiday activities and the long workdays, I didn't even have time to unpack and get settled in my new condo.

Late on Friday night, January 22, I unpacked one of the last moving boxes. It contained books.

I was very tired and decided I'd put them away the next evening. I piled them on the dining room table and went to bed.

The next morning, I got ready to leave for work. My purse was lying on the table. As I reached to pick it up, I noticed that on top of the pile of books I had unpacked the night before, was my old copy of *This Is Earl Nightingale*.

"Hmmm . . . maybe I'll just take this along and have him sign it," I smiled.

Chapter 5

*There is nothing holier, in this life of ours,
than the first consciousness of love –
the first fluttering of its silken wings.*
                    H. W. Longfellow (1839)

Later, Earl wrote:

In January of 1982, I was in Punta Gorda, Florida, where I was in partnership with my good friend, Don Donelson. We'd been friends on the other coast.

When Don moved to Punta Gorda, he asked me to come over and do some commercials for his development at Emerald Point. I agreed. When I went over, I liked what I saw and bought a villa next to his.

One day while I was poking about an area that had once been an old fishing pier, it occurred to me that this would make a great location for a good restaurant. (Earl loved good food and fine dining and was often disappointed in service and food.)

So, we went to the city and got a ninety-nine year lease on the pier and built some first-class shops at ground level and some really fine apartments above them; then, at the end, we built the Earl Nightingale Restaurant – a real five-star restaurant with a spectacular view of Charlotte Harbor and the yacht basin.

So anyway, I was in town and Don asked me to address the Saturday morning sales meeting. It wasn't something I really wanted to do, I was still recovering from heart surgery; but felt I should, and so I agreed.

It was my first month on the job. And I had begun to look forward to this Saturday meeting, as Mac had predicted. He was going to distribute bonus checks at the meeting. Mine was sure to be hefty; I was tops in sales.

We were a sales staff of 30. Three of us were women, much to the chagrin of the company trainer. He thought all women should be home doing dishes. And he made no bones about it.

He responded to my instant, unfathomable success with off-handed respect. It became a verbal weapon with which he brow beat the men who had allowed me to outperform them.

Bonus check Saturday finally arrived, featuring Earl Nightingale. He didn't look anything like the man I had seen in the photos and videos. He wore a pair of faded jeans, a sport shirt, no tie, a leather jacket, a beard and mustache. He appeared tired. He spoke to our group briefly on goals and wished us well.

When the meeting ended, I walked toward Earl with the book Phil had given me years earlier.

"Mr. Nightingale, I've had this beat-up old book for a number of years now. Will you do me the honor of signing it?" I asked.

That next few minutes will be forever frozen in my mind, as I remember the expression on his face. Although his face appeared very tired, there was a twinkle in those blue eyes.

He stood there smiling at me, as though he recognized an old friend in the crowd. He took my book and asked softly, "Are you married?"

"No," I replied. "Just make it out to Diana."

He stood there smiling, as though waiting for me to say something else. Finally, he said, "Would you like to be?"

What kind of a stupid, fresh question was that, I wondered. I felt uncomfortable. Since I always respond to an uncomfortable situation with a joke, I dryly asked, "What's that, the Ben Franklin close?"

His response was so quick, you would have thought our dialogue had been rehearsed. "No, it's called asking for the sale." He grinned from ear to ear, autographed my book and handed it back.

I thanked him, left the salesroom and went to work.

About noon, I finally got a break. When I returned to the reception area, the rest of the sales staff was standing around, as if they were waiting for a parade or an important announcement. But all eyes were on me.

"Earl Nightingale came in and asked to see you. You're supposed to call him right away, as soon as possible – in Villa Number One." The receptionist was very excited and smiling. Now, there was silence in the room.

"Okay, thanks," I said and turned to leave.

"Aren't you going to call him? He wanted you to call him right away. Do you want me to ring his villa for you?" she pressed.

"No," I said. "I need to do a couple of things. I'll call him later."

"But he said, 'As soon as possible.' He's probably waiting for your call."

"Yeah, I'll bet he's up there just holding his breath." I laughed at how ridiculous the idea sounded. "I'd better call him."

I tried to find a place to talk privately; but my inquisitive friends were huddled around me.

I instantly recognized Earl's famous voice. He said he had been impressed by my recognition checks and my Salesperson of the Month Award. He said my bosses were trying to clone me, because I was doing such a great job. He asked if I would have dinner with him that evening.

I told Earl I had plans for that evening and that I had the next day off, the first in a long time. But I said I would be happy to have dinner with him Monday after work, if that worked for him. He sounded delighted. We exchanged a few more pleasantries and I hung up. My sales buddies were grinning and poking each other. Then the ribbing began.

"Look, you yahoos," I said. "If you were tops in sales this month, Earl Nightingale would be taking you out to dinner instead of me. He probably wants to know how I manage to out-sell all of you guys."

That weekend, I contracted one hellacious cold. By Monday I was congested, blowing my nose and coughing my head off. That evening, I was a mess. I met Earl for drinks in the lounge of Earl Nightingale's Restaurant. From the moment I sat down, I felt comfortable, as though I was joining an old friend.

Conversation came easily for us and we skipped immediately to the intimacies of our lives; where we'd been, what we'd done. We talked about our children as though the other had known each of them intimately since birth.

By the time we sat down to dinner, we were best buddies. We talked about everything from professional success to personal failure in our marriages to raising children. We laughed and talked. We shared a mud pie for dessert.

I appeared to make a miraculous recovery from my cold and felt great.

Earl had a problem, and asked for my help. There was a woman reporter who wanted an interview with him. He was willing to be interviewed; but she insisted upon conducting it over dinner. He'd finally, agreed to meet her Wednesday evening.

"That kind of woman makes me nervous," he confided. "I think she wants more than an interview. Will you come along and protect me?"

I laughed and said I'd be happy to.

"Don't leave me alone with her, promise?" He flashed a conspiratorial smile.

"I promise."

Wednesday evening, I left work at six o'clock and went to Earl's villa. The reporter was already there and "dressed for bear." Earl and I exchanged knowing smiles when he opened the door.

We'd each had a drink and were preparing to leave for the restaurant, when the reporter walked over to the kitchen counter and poured herself another.

"There isn't time," Earl said. "I've made reservations, and we should really be leaving."

She gave him a seductive look and said, "I'll just put it in the refrigerator and have it later."

Earl looked at me with sheer panic.

Dinner turned out to be fun. Earl and I had managed to disarm the reporter, who turned out to be very nice after all. She kept the interview brief and commented about how nice it must be for old friends like us to be together again.

When the evening ended, Earl and I walked her to her car and waved goodbye. We chatted as we walked to my car. I unlocked the door.

"Thanks, pal," he said, and shook my hand. I nodded, thanked him for a fun evening, got in the car and drove away.

The next morning, Earl called the office and told me his son and a date were driving over from Fort Lauderdale the following day. He very much wanted me to meet Tad. I agreed to drop by after work. Next, Earl wanted to know if I would go to lunch with him. I explained that we didn't break for lunch. We were too busy and usually just grabbed a bite in the back room between guests.

He said, "It's OK. I'll just tell Don. He won't mind."

I begged off. I was having enough trouble with the other staff members because of our dinners. Lunch would not be a good idea. I'd see him the next evening.

Friday was hectic. I was glad to see the day end and looked forward to getting home early. I had planned to keep my visit with Earl brief because I was relapsing from my cold and needed to rest.

Earl was on the phone when I arrived. He was talking with his daughter, Pam, in Carmel. He introduced me to Tad and his friend and resumed his conversation. Tad was a handsome young man and very personable. We continued talking while Earl happily chatted on the phone.

After a few minutes, Tad talked with his sister; then Earl got back on the line. Earl was saying that someone was wonderful – the girl of his dreams – and he'd found her right there in Punta Gorda of all places. He couldn't wait for Pam to meet her.

"You'll love her! She's great. No, I don't know. But she's a grandmother and she's terrific."

A few more exchanges and he said, "Diana, come and say hello to Pam. I've told her all about you and she's dying to meet you."

Pam and I spoke briefly. I was a little confused – actually I was quite confused! She sounded as though her father and I were having some sort of a relationship, when in reality we had only shared two meals. Our intimacy level was restricted to some intense and intimate discussions about our lives. That was it.

As Earl hung up the phone, I grabbed my purse to leave and said it was nice to have met Tad.

"You can't go," Earl said. "We're all going to dinner."

"I've made other plans," I said. "I really can't. You didn't say anything about dinner and I promised my daughter, Jill, that we'd do something special tonight. We don't see much of each other with our crazy schedules. I just can't."

Little did I know that Earl, like my mother, never accepted negative responses. Especially, *I can't.*

"Of course you can! Call home and explain to Jill that I'm going back to California in the morning and this is the only night we can get together."

"I really can't," I said.

"Pick up the phone and call," Earl insisted.

I dialed my number.

Jill answered, "Oh, Mom, I'm so glad you called! I know this is supposed to be our special night. But I want to spend the night at Tracey's. You don't mind, do you, Mom? We can do something another night. Okay, Mom? Please?"

"Well, sure, if that's what you'd rather do – "

"Thanks, Mom, you're wonderful. Call you in the morning. Bye."

"Bye." I stood there, feeling as if I had just been sideswiped. I was living my life at the whim of my teenaged child. I turned to Earl.

"It's okay," I said, "I fixed it."

It was a lovely dinner. Tad was humorous, intelligent and a delight to be with. After dessert and coffee, Tad and his date left. They had a long drive back to the other coast, and it was getting late. Earl and I lingered over bottomless cups of coffee until we were the last ones in the restaurant.

Finally, realizing everyone there wanted to go home, Earl asked for the check. It was late, the restaurant was dim, candles burned on the tables, music played. Earl was signing the check and said in a rather matter-of-fact voice, "I have a goal, you know."

"I can't imagine Earl Nightingale without one," I chuckled.

"Want to know what it is?"

I hadn't known Earl long; but I knew him well enough to know he'd tell me, whether or not I wanted to know.

"To make you my wife," he said, as he looked up.

I sank back in my chair. I remembered what he'd said when I asked him to autograph my book. Now after three dinners, it looked like we'd gone full circle.

"If this man makes a cheap pass at me now, I will be painfully disappointed in him," I thought.

"You think I'm kidding or something, don't you? Well, I'm not. I'm dead serious."

I could see, even in the dimly lit room, looking into those blue eyes, that he was dead serious.

"I've been looking for you all of my life. The other morning when I saw you at the meeting, I knew you were the one. I've searched the faces of thousands of women in every airport, every audience and every place I've gone — looking.

"Last Saturday, I found the woman I've been in love with and looking for all these years. I knew it in an instant."

Those were the words I had said to my mom just two weeks earlier. Now they echoed through my brain and I felt like I was having a stroke or some sort of out-of-body experience.

I could hear the blood pulsating up one side of my neck, up over my head and down the other side. I was speechless. I couldn't move. I just sat there – staring at him.

"I'll give you time to get used to the idea," Earl was saying.

"Wait a minute," I fumbled. "Didn't you hear anything I've been saying to you this week? Remember, I said I like my life the way it is? I love my work. I have goals and plans – and none of them includes a man or marriage."

Earl just smiled, his eyes twinkling.

"Look, don't take this personally," I went on. "But I don't want to marry you or anyone else right now. I especially don't want to marry a person in the public eye. I'm a very private person. I have an unlisted number and I don't give it out. When I'm home, I don't want to hear from anyone, unless I *want* to hear from them.

"Besides, I love my work. And I just bought a new condo. And I have a daughter who's a junior in high school and can't be disrupted. And I don't want to move away, especially to California, and leave my life here. And — " I'd finally run out of reasons. "I'm sorry, but I could never marry you!" I blurted.

Earl sat there with a patient look; the kind of look you'd give a five-year old who's telling you what she thinks is news — but you already know the outcome of the story.

Earl was very calm, very serious. "Yes, well, I'll give you a chance to get used to the idea. But you are the one I've been looking for."

He smiled and slowly rose from his chair. I couldn't move. He helped me from my chair, took my arm, led me from the restaurant and headed for my car.

"Do you live far from the airport?" Earl asked.

"Not really. Ten, fifteen minutes, maybe. Why?"

"I leave at seven in the morning and if you were up – Will you be up?"

How strange, I thought. Now we're talking about airports.

"Oh, sure, Saturday morning meeting, remember?"

"Well, if you were up and came by to see me off, it sure would mean a lot to me."

He'd stopped talking about me being `the one'.

I was relieved. "Sure, I'll see you then."

We had reached my car by now. Earl leaned over and kissed me on the forehead.

"See you in the morning."

The 35-mile drive home was a blur, as I tried to sort out what had happened. When did I give him the impression I was even remotely interested in him in *that* way? I tried thinking about marrying him. I couldn't even begin to imagine it. Impossible!

Well, good thing he'd be gone in the morning. There'll be more than 3-thousand miles between us and this will all be over.

The next morning I got up, showered, pulled on a sweat shirt, jeans and sneakers. I figured I'd come home, put on my make-up and get dressed for work after the plane left.

The traffic was light and I arrived at little Page Field Airport in Fort Myers in nothing flat. Earl was very happy to see me. (He told me after we were married that if there had been one shred of doubt in his mind I was the right one, my arrival that morning at the airport erased it.)

Earl talked nervously about the length of the flight, that he'd fly into San Francisco and then catch a commuter to Monterey. I was nodding and smiling. It was time to board.

We walked to the security gate and Earl turned to me and said, "Well, I'll look forward to the day when you join me in Carmel."

"You don't even have my telephone number. It's unlisted, remember?"

"I stole it out of the files in the office," he said with a grin. He leaned forward, kissed me on the cheek, passed through security and was gone.

Again, I was frozen in place. I shook my head, went out into the morning sun mumbling under my breath, sighed and drove home.

What a week it had been and what a wild experience. I certainly couldn't tell anyone about it. Who'd believe it?

One thing for sure, he was a neat guy. And regardless of how the week had ended, wherever we went in the world and whatever we did in years to come, I knew we'd be close friends.

Jill was prone in front of the television when I returned home that evening. She and Tracey had stayed up most of the night. She wanted to know if I'd brought dinner. I hadn't, but said we'd go for pizza. I looked for the mail.

"It's by the phone. Oh yeah, there was a phone call for you from some man with a deep, unusual voice. He called from California. He said you should call him right away, no matter what time you got home. The number's there by the phone."

That was January 30, 1982. Earl called every day after that. He was right. After a while, I began to get "used to the idea".

Chapter 6

Love is the tyrant of the heart;
it darkens reason, confounds discretion;
deaf to counsel,
It runs a headlong course to desperate madness.
                                    John Ford (1628)

Mother went back to Ohio a few days after I met Earl. I had told her all about him addressing the meeting, about him autographing my book and that I was going to have dinner with him. She didn't think she had ever heard of Earl Nightingale, so she wasn't impressed. However, if he was as famous as I said he was, she found it odd that he would ask me to dinner.

Several months had passed. It was March 25th. I was leaving for Carmel that afternoon. By now, Mother knew all about Earl and listened faithfully every day to his radio program, *Our Changing World.*

But she was mostly impressed that he had been the radio voice of Sky King. She found it ironic that she and I had listened to him together when I was a little girl. I think she got caught up in his role as Sky, the mature hero and uncle of Clipper and Penny; forgetting altogether that he actually had been a very young man, himself, at the time.

Mom, being a mom, still viewed Earl as a stranger – a male stranger. And she wasn't at all happy that I was flying off to stay with him at his home. I told her that Earl's partner, Lloyd Conant, and his wife, Hazel, were house guests. So, we would be properly chaperoned. I also assured her that I had a round trip ticket and promised to jump on the first plane home if I needed to.

What Mom didn't need to know were all the details of what had happened since she left Florida and Earl had returned home.

Yes, he'd called the same day he left Florida and everyday since. And yes, I was beginning to get used to the "idea." But, my whole life had changed because of his calls.

At first, out of consideration, I would be sure to be home to receive his long distance call. I'd postpone activities until after our scheduled talks. As time passed, I found I looked forward to his calls and didn't want to go anywhere or do anything after; but instead, would spend hours thinking about our conversations.

Earl called every day without fail. He'd tell me what he had for lunch, with whom he'd talked, what he had written that day, his plans for dinner, where he was going. He generally gave me an hour-by-hour itinerary of his plans.

At the beginning of March, Earl was very excited. His partner and his partner's wife were coming from Chicago, to help celebrate Earl's birthday, which was on the 12th. His upcoming birthday was very important to him. With his new heart valve, he had a good long life expectancy. Now that he'd found the girl of his dreams, life was full of hope and he was ready to celebrate, big time.

The day before his birthday, Earl told me Lloyd and Hazel had arrived and they were going to dinner later. The 12th came and went. The first day without a call from Earl. While I thought it strange, I suspected that they had decided to drive to San Francisco or down the coast sightseeing. I was sure I'd hear from him soon.

Days passed, then a week. This was strange. I'd gotten to know Earl and this wasn't like him. I phoned the house; no answer. I called his office; no answer. I called early. I called late. There could be only one reason. They must be away. But then I'd tell myself that he would call me no matter where he was or what he was doing.

I stayed busy, even workng on days off. I kept busy; but I was always mentally connected to Earl, wondering where he was. The evening of the 24th, I directed my energy toward my housework, something I'd neglected while I was maintaining my lead in the sales race at work.

I took a shower, went to bed, read for a while, talked to God and went to sleep.

Just before dawn, I was awakened by what I thought was Earl's voice, shouting my name. I sat up, wet with perspiration and filled with fear. I knew it wasn't a dream. Earl was in trouble and he needed me. I got up, made a pot of tea and waited for it to be seven o'clock in California.

The morning dragged. Finally, I called. The phone rang twice and an unfamiliar voice answered the phone. It was Earl's partner, Lloyd. He said it was a miracle that I was calling. Earl was in the hospital and Lloyd couldn't find my number anywhere. Earl was heavily medicated and couldn't remember my number. But he kept asking for me.

Without asking for details, I told Lloyd that I'd be on the next plane west. I'd call him with my arrival time.

I quickly called my boss, Don. After I explained to him what little I knew, we agreed I should get to the west coast as soon as possible. I arranged to have Jill stay with her father's mom, who lived nearby.

I boarded the red-eye to San Francisco, arriving in the wee hours of the morning; too late to fly to Monterey. I spent the night at the airport Sheraton and took the commuter to Monterey the next morning. I remember sitting on the plane, staring out the window at the mountains below, knowing this trip would change my life forever — no matter what the outcome.

Lloyd and Hazel met me at the airport. There was much to tell. I heard the words and understood what I was being told; but my heart didn't believe the story. Something wasn't right.

Lloyd said Earl had told him how much he loved me. And, Earl had told him we'd be married soon.

On his birthday, Earl kept expecting me to show up and surprise him. That evening, he had lingered at home before going to dinner; waiting, hoping. They'd had drinks and waited. Finally they left, with Earl believing that I'd show up at the restaurant.

They'd had wine with dinner; and afterward, more drinks. Earl was feeling no pain when it was time to go home.

As they left the restaurant, Earl spotted a huge boulder in the middle of the garden. He laughingly said he knew it was a *magic rock* and he was going to sit on it. If he wished hard enough, he said, it would split open and I would appear.

Lloyd said it was apparent to him that Earl had *"lost it."* So with Hazel's help, he put the inebriated and disappointed Earl in the car and took him to a nearby hospital to be admitted.

Upon arrival, Earl became aggressive. He insisted there was nothing wrong with him and said he was not going to stay there. He was sedated; and, at Lloyd's instruction, admitted for observation in the pavilion for patients with emotional illnesses.

A week had passed. Lloyd said he didn't know what to do with Earl, and was glad I was there. We drove to the hospital.

Lloyd had arranged to have Earl leave for a "visit." I waited in the car with Hazel while Lloyd went inside. Earl came out of the hospital looking old, tired and defeated. I got out of the car and ran toward him. He put his arms around me, held me tightly and cried.

There was something wrong; not with Earl, as far as I could tell. But something wasn't right. I just couldn't put my finger on it.

Lloyd suggested that we go to lunch. I was much more interested in working on a plan to get Earl out of that hospital. Going to lunch and behaving as if everything was normal seemed inappropriate, when there seemed to be so much for us to figure out.

When we returned to Earl's house, he asked to be alone with me. So we went for a walk on the golf course, past Quail Lodge, hand in hand along the path under the pepper trees. We talked non-stop. Earl was both sad about his present predicament and happy I finally was there.

As we walked, I began to feel something strange, but familiar. I felt safe, at home. This was the feeling I'd dreamed about when I was just a little girl; a feeling of belonging.

I stopped, turned and faced Earl. "All of my life I have been restless, in a hurry to go or be somewhere but not knowing quite what it was I was rushing off to or from. I often felt like I was being driven by some unseen force, like a person just a little out of control. Now, just now, I know! I was supposed to be here – with you."

In that moment, I knew for certain that I had always been on my way to Earl. And I knew I'd never leave his side, ever again. We returned home, happy to be together at last and excited about the future.

Lloyd insisted that Earl return to the hospital for treatment. I argued that he should return for one reason -- for his doctors to release him.

We tried to set up an appointment with his doctors, but they weren't available. We'd have to wait until the next day. I told Earl I would be at his home. And if he needed me for anything, he should call me and I'd be there in a heartbeat.

On the drive back to Earl's, Lloyd and Hazel announced that they were going to return to Chicago later that day. I didn't understand. They'd put Earl in that hospital. Weren't they going to make sure he got out OK?

Lloyd said he needed to get back to the office. He was sure I would work things out with the doctors. I drove them to the airport and, armed with a map of the Monterey Peninsula as my only guide, I headed back to Carmel.

I checked Earl's refrigerator for food. There wasn't any. I checked the pantry. Nothing there either. The only thing that was well stocked was the bar. Interesting, I thought. I made a list. Then, map in hand, I found my way to the grocery store, where I filled a cart with every healthy thing I could find.

With the trunk full, I went back in and bought pots of chrysanthemums and stuffed them into the back seat.

I then headed home, with the only ammunition I had to save Earl: flowers, music, food and lots of love.

Earl called that evening. He was concerned about his health. Since his heart surgery, he said, there were times he just didn't feel right. Maybe Lloyd was right to hospitalize him, he thought.

I told him not to think about things like that. He, of all people, knew the power of thoughts. He needed to think and believe that everything was going to be just fine.

I asked him if he thought he'd be able to rest that night. He said he'd try. Someone there was having a birthday and they were going to celebrate later with ice cream and cake. He thought that would make the evening pass faster.

The next morning, Earl called very early. He said he was very excited about coming home and felt better than he had in a long time. He said he hadn't been able to sleep after the party.

As he lay in bed, he thought about all the dirty dishes they'd left for the cleaning staff. He said the woman who usually came in the morning was very elderly.

She reminded him of his mother in her later years. He remembered how hard Honey had worked to raise him and his brothers. How sad, he thought, to see someone her age having to clean up other people's messes to earn a living.

So, since he couldn't sleep, he decided to wash the dishes for her. I thought that was really sweet and told him so.

I showered, went to the kitchen and started a big pot of Greek stew. I had bread rising on the counter, pots of flowers all over the house, had started a fire in the gas fireplaces, and had filled the house with music.

I drove to the hospital and parked in the patient loading area out front. I wasn't out of the car yet, when a nurse rushed out to meet me.

"Are you here to pick up Mr. Nightingale?"

"Yes, I am. Is it okay to park here?"

"Well, there's been a mistake. Mr. Nightingale isn't being released. Mr. Conant admitted him. And until we've completed our evaluation, he's not going anywhere."

At that moment, I became someone I'd never known before. I stormed out of the car. I pushed past the nurse, rushed up to the desk and demanded to see the doctor, *immediately.*

The woman behind the desk wasn't sure he was available. I insisted that he was – and if he wasn't, I'd call the newspapers and the police.

Thinking back, it's surprising they didn't lock me up. I was totally out of control. Instead, they showed me to a small therapy room where Earl sat, obviously deeply sedated. This was not the man I had spoken with earlier that morning.

The doctor entered and sat between Earl and me. He spoke in patronizing tones. Mr. Nightingale couldn't go anywhere, he explained. Mr. Nightingale was unstable, perhaps even violent. I needed protection from him.

I couldn't believe what I was hearing. I was furious. What, if any, authority did he have to hold Earl there, I demanded to know. Did Lloyd have power of attorney over Earl? Where were the papers that gave Lloyd any legal right at all to institutionalize Earl?

Still smiling, still cajoling, the doctor responded. "My dear, you just don't know what danger you're in. This man is not rational. Do you know what he did this morning? He *washed dishes!* What do you think of that?"

"I think that was a very thoughtful and caring thing to do. Anything else?" I retorted.

"Well, there was the rock incident at the restaurant, when he thought it was magical."

I looked at Earl. He was so sad. I smiled, never taking my eyes off of him and said, "It *is* a magical rock. He thought that if he sat on it and believed hard enough, I'd appear. And he was right. I'm here. Now, sign his release papers. I'm taking him home."

"But, surely – "

"Now!"

The doctor stood up, angry now. "I hope you won't live to regret this, Madam. If you get him home and he becomes violent, you'll be sorry –"

"No. I'll be surprised."

I got up, walked over to Earl and said, "Come on, we're going home."

The days and weeks that followed were lived in absolute blind faith. I believed that Earl was a well man and treated him as such. Now, all we had to do was figure out what was preventing his physical body from echoing my belief.

First, we made a list of his doctors and made appointments with each of them. We also made lists of the medications each had prescribed for him without input from the others. We began to map out what we believed could be wrong. It didn't take long.

Earl's body was the battlefield for chemical warfare. There had never been a consultation between the different physicians, no common game plan for medication. So Earl was taking handfuls of incompatible prescription drugs morning, noon, and night. Some of the combinations could have killed him. No one told him not to drink alcohol with them. No wonder he thought I would appear from a rock.

It wasn't long before we got his medications balanced and Earl felt better than ever before. We'd get up every morning and set out on new adventures; driving up or down the California coast or going inland to find wonderful Mexican restaurants and shops. We took long walks, sat at the beach and watched the sunsets; then came home to sit by the fire at night to talk.

One evening, Earl and I were having dinner and he asked me once again to marry him. This time, I knew he was serious and I knew my answer was yes.

I was anxious to call my mother and tell her we were setting a date. We talked regularly. And by now she was properly impressed that I was having a serious relationship with Sky King.

"Mom, Earl asked me to marry him tonight at dinner and I said yes. Mom? Are you there?"

"Yes, yes, of course I'm here. I'm just thinking – marrying Earl Nightingale. Why, he's a famous man."

"Yes, Mom, he is."

"He's on the radio all over the world. Everybody knows him."

"Yes, Mom that's true."

"Why, he could marry anyone in the whole world."

"Yes, Mom."

"Well, what in the world does he want with you?"

That was Mother.

"Let me put Earl on the phone, Mom. Maybe he can explain it to you."

They had become friends by phone through our weeks of conversation. Now, he was listening in on the extension in the bedroom and laughing like crazy.

He interrupted, "Mother, I've been looking for Diana all of my life. Of course, I didn't know who she was or what her name was, but I knew she was out there all the same. I just kept a picture of her, the way I knew she'd be, in my mind and in my heart; knowing that one day I'd find her. I looked, and made a couple of false attempts and knew they were not right when I was making them. But even then, I knew I would find her one day.

"You know, Mother, I'm 61 years old. And I've been successful at everything I've touched. But life hasn't had much meaning without my Diana at my side to share it all with.

"I've been through numerous health problems. And recently, after my heart surgery, I hit a particularly low spot in my life. There have been times when I've driven down the coast between Carmel and Big Sur and felt so lost that I wanted to drive my car off the cliff. But, I wasn't a quitter. I believed that I would find her, if I just hung in there long enough. And sure enough, at that Saturday morning meeting that neither of us wanted to attend, there she was.

"I love her very much. And I'll take good care of her."

He hung up. Mother was crying, I was crying. Earl came into the kitchen. He was crying.

Chapter 7

*Come live with me and be my love,
And we will all the pleasure prove,
That valleys, groves, or hills or fields,
Or woods and steepy mountains yield."*
                    Christopher Marlowe (1599)

After Earl's recovery and return to work, things got back to normal between us and the Conants. They were delighted with our plans; especially when they learned that our wedding date was also their 38th anniversary. We asked them to make it extra special by being our witnesses.

It would be a small wedding. Earl and I had spent long hours talking about the kind of ceremony we wanted.

The logistics were overwhelming. Five of our six children were out of state; as were our brothers, my sisters and mother. It would be difficult to plan to have everyone come to California; to say nothing of the cost. Then there were close friends; all of mine out of state. It just seemed too complicated. What we really wanted was something private and simple.

We already had spoken with a judge in Monterey, who'd agreed to perform the ceremony at the house. We pared the event down to the five of us and decided to say our vows in the rose garden.

The Conants arrived a day or two before the wedding. It was a good time for all of us.

On the big day, Hazel and I took off after breakfast to have our hair done. Actually, Hazel got her hair done. Mine had been "done in" a few days earlier, when I trusted my wedding coif to one of Carmel's creative hair geniuses. He all but shaved my head. My hair was about two inches long on top and shorter still on the sides. If my bangs had been longer, I could have spiked them and been an early punker.

I had burst into tears when I saw what he had done. But, cry as I may, I was stuck with a boy cut for my big day. In final desperation, I lightly sprayed what was left and inserted tiny sprigs of baby's breath.

Hazel and I returned home around noon to pick up our guys for an early lunch. Neither Earl nor I ate much, and were anxious to get back to the house. The judge was due a little before three.

As the afternoon progressed, our moods became more serious. We moved about the house slowly and dressed in silence. I walked toward Earl's bedroom. He was standing in front of his dresser, putting his things in his pockets.

I asked him if he was nervous. He said he was so nervous that he felt like he was going to throw up. He said he'd waited a very long time for this day. It was the most important day of his life.

The only other time he was that nervous, he recalled, was when he was about to speak to a packed house at Carnegie Hall. He was awed by the responsibility of giving that audience something valuable to take away with them. Now, he said, he hoped he could give me something of value for the trust I was placing in him.

He turned to look at me, took my hands in his and said, "Honey, I don't know what lies ahead for us. I hope we have years and years together. But maybe we won't. So let's, from this day forward, have width to compensate — in case we don't get length. Let's try and have it all. I do know one thing for sure, and I promise you this – life with me will never be boring."

When the judge arrived, we greeted him and showed him around the house. Then, as we would with any guest, retired to the kitchen. We exchanged small talk. He talked about being a fan of Earl's. Finally, we got around to discussing the wedding.

We wanted to audiotape the ceremony, so we could share it with our friends and family who couldn't be there. The judge suggested that we go to the garden to see where we wanted to stand, and find a place for the tape recorder.

The day couldn't have been more beautiful. There was a clear, deep blue sky with white puffy clouds. A hummingbird was flitting from rose to rose.

The judge moved us around. When he felt we were placed properly, he laid the tape recorder at our feet.

"Let's give this a try," he said, satisfied that everything was just right.

Just then, our neighbor across the street fired up his power mower. The sound of it filled the air. The judge raised his voice louder and began shouting his lines. We shouted back in the appropriate places. Finally, he said, "I now pronounce you Man and Wife!"

We just stood there a second, waiting to be told if that was a good rehearsal.

Then the judge said, "Earl, don't you want to kiss your bride?" We stood there, dumbfounded. Then, we realized what he had said. That was no rehearsal. It – it was over. We'd taken our vows, not to the music of an organ or a choir, but to the whine of a lawn mower!

After a moment or two, we realized how funny it was and we all burst out laughing. Then we hugged, kissed and shed happy tears. We gathered up our recorder and went inside where it was quiet.

As we opened the champagne, the doorbell rang. Answering the door we found a florist with the largest bouquet of roses I had ever seen in my life.

It may not have been what most people would consider a romantic start. But we thought it was just great. We were happy – and best of all, we were married.

We celebrated at home awhile, then drove down Ocean Avenue, to park at the beach. The sunset that evening was glorious. No fog, just beautiful clouds in a sky of red, orange, purple, silver and gold above a deep blue sea with white crashing waves.

We drove back up the road to the Pine Inn where a special table had been reserved for our little wedding party. Our waiter highly recommended the duck that evening and promised it would be special. I was the only one to order it.

And it certainly was special. I think they started baking it when we'd made our reservations days earlier, because it was like paper.

When I put my fork in it, it crumbled away like a cracker. I didn't mind, I really wasn't very hungry.

A couple who knew Earl stopped by our table to wish us well. They were anxious to know how we'd met. So we invited them to join us for a drink while Earl told the story, his wonderful voice making the adventure sound even more wonderful than one could imagine. He held my hand and smiled at me and finished the story with tears in his eyes as he leaned over and kissed me. Everyone at the table was crying and blowing their noses. The couple got up to leave and said, "It's just like a fairy tale!"

In reality it was – just like a fairy tale. Funny, how people think of fairy tales in romantic terms. The prince meets the maiden. They fall in love, ride off into the sunset and live happily ever after. But think about what usually occurs between "Once upon a time," and "they lived happily ever after."

There are countless villains, life-threatening circumstances and challenges beyond the wildest imagination. We certainly had our share. As Earl used to say, "It ain't all beer and skittles."

We'd already had our share of life-threatening challenges in the previous months. We clearly were ready for "happily ever after."

The next morning about seven-thirty, Earl came into the bedroom.

"This is a fine kettle of fish," he announced in a very serious tone. We had guests, and the lady of the house was still sleeping.

Our guests' body clocks were operating two time zones ahead of ours. In addition, they were early risers.

They had fixed coffee and juice for themselves. And now, I was hearing about it. I leaped out of bed, threw on my robe and went out to the family room.

Still sleepy-eyed, I stood there getting oriented to my surroundings. Any evidence of the previous day's celebration was gone. The TV was on, with the national news blaring. Spreadsheets covered the table and counters. Lloyd was on the phone to Chicago. I still trying to get my bearings when he hung up.

"We've been up for hours." He was looking at me as though I had screwed up, my first day on the job. There was no "Good morning," no smile, just disapproval.

I walked over to the refrigerator and poured myself a glass of juice and tried to laugh it off.

"Sorry I wasn't up to fix your coffee. I guess I thought I was on my honeymoon. Apparently there's been a mix up here."

"Well, we did expect you'd be up –" he said.

"I'm sorry, I didn't know you'd be up so early," I said apologetically. "I guess I figured you'd take care of yourselves. I've never been in a situation where adults waited to be taken care of by other adults.

"You and Earl have known each other for so long, and have lived together on so many occasions. I'd think you'd be more at home here than I, and would just fix yourself anything you want – just as you did all the years before I came along; and as you have done all week long.

"I had no idea that everything would change overnight, once Earl and I were married."

I drank my juice and fought back the tears. I wasn't a morning person to begin with. And I was hurt and angry that everything had changed so abruptly overnight. Yesterday, they took care of themselves. Today, they expected me to wait on them. Yesterday we had been friends, family. Now, I didn't know what they expected of me.

Before the wedding, the first one up made coffee. Later, we'd go to breakfast. Then, it hit me. Lloyd and Hazel were playing a practical joke! I searched for clues in their faces. They were neither joking nor cared that I was upset.

I returned Lloyd's impatient gaze, "When shall I anticipate the arrival of The Handbook?" I asked.

"What handbook?"

"The one that contains the rules and regulations I'm expected to follow as Mrs. Earl Nightingale."

He began to laugh nervously, shocked that I'd talk to him that way. I'm sure Hazel never dared to do that. She was a sweet lady.

I left the room and returned to the master suite to shower. I was shaking and angry and bitterly disappointed. So much for a romance-filled honeymoon. Earl came in behind me, grinning from ear to ear.

"That's my girl – you're going to have to be tough. People are going to try and walk all over you and test you every bit of the way. You're terrific, a real fighter. And to think, I've got you in my corner. I'm a lucky guy."

He had his arms around me and I knew he meant his words as praise. But, I was scared to death. I knew from that first morning, being his wife wasn't going to be easy. But it wasn't nearly as hard as I had imagined it would be that day.

Chapter 8

*True love always involves renunciation
of one's personal comfort.*
                    Lyof N. Tolstoy (1887)

Earl was 61 when we met. He had been a rebel since childhood and was still a free spirit. So it was easy for us to understand and identify with each other's strong mind and will.

Shortly after we were married, our independent personalities collided. As is the case most often, the issue wasn't important. I don't even remember what it was all about.

No one was wrong. We were both right. But we both knew the handling of this conflict would be critical to our relationship, because each of us believed that giving in would mean relinquishing our personal integrity and perhaps set the pattern for all future confrontations. That day was extremely long and painfully quiet.

That night, as we got into bed, it was difficult to fight back the tears. I lay in the darkness, hardly breathing. I knew I couldn't find the words to define my thoughts and feelings. I wanted to say something. But I didn't want another confrontation. I wanted it resolved before sleep and thought that maybe if I just touched his shoulder – I reached out, and he was reaching to touch me. He put his arms around me and we held each other in silence, knowing then that our love was greater than any of our differences.

In the morning, we discussed our feelings and knew that we'd always find a way to compromise without either of us giving up our individual beliefs.

The experience, coupled with our love and trust, fortified the wonderful foundation upon which we built the remainder of our life together.

Earl's constant love, understanding and support never ceased to humble me during my most difficult times. And I seemed to have a lot of them; because those first years, being married to a public figure, were indeed difficult for me.

A very strong sense of humor saved us from many a bad situation, too. It kept us from taking ourselves too seriously — and just going mad when individuals were rude or thoughtless.

We loved being together and were always arm in arm, heads together, sharing thoughts and secrets. A week didn't go by that someone wouldn't walk up to us, step between us, push me out of the way and want Earl for themselves.

When I wasn't with Earl, local merchants, waitresses, a maitre d' would say, "Oh, Mrs. Nightingale — of course! I didn't recognize you without your husband."

Or, "Mrs. Nightingale, will you please move out of the way so that we can take a picture of Mr. Nightingale?"

Or the one I loved most, "Mrs. Nightingale, will you please take a picture of us with Mr. Nightingale?"

Usually, when a woman marries, she becomes Mrs. John Doe, unless she marries a public figure in which case she simply becomes invisible. If a man marries a famous woman, instead of remaining Mr. John Doe, he also becomes invisible.

When we were traveling, if someone acknowledged me at all, it was generally, "So, are you enjoying shopping while your husband is here working?"

I threatened to write a book titled, *I Don't Shop*; a manual for people who say dumb things. I hoped to help them understand what it feels like to be the spouse of a famous person.

Long before you relinquish your individuality, you are stripped of your anonymity. No meal, vacation, trip to the grocery store or hospital ever was taken without someone invading our privacy.

Most times, it was enjoyable. Fans are indeed wonderful people. They are very important people. Without them to applaud, the works of artists would go unknown and unappreciated.

Being in the public eye also affords an opportunity to meet wonderful people you would never have met otherwise. And for the most part, the majority of the people you get to know are a real blessing. Every now and then however, there is another, frightening kind of person who shows up, takes the joy out of your work and fills you with a gripping fear.

There was one particular kind of man who unnerved me in every situation and every city we met him.

He was the man who failed to see Earl as a successful businessman; but instead saw only The Legend. He would come to worship at Earl's feet, and believed that no woman was good enough for this Legend.

This type of man always behaved the same. First, he would stand at a distance and observe the Legend, surrounded by his adoring fans. As he watched, he would become more agitated and impatient with the others — and most especially, with me.

Finally, after everyone was through asking for autographs, he would come forth, tell Earl how wonderful he was and then turn to me and in an ugly voice say, "I just hope you realize how *lucky* you are to be married to this wonderful man."

It was as if they'd read the same script. It never deviated. After a while, I became agitated and sometimes a little frightened by them. But I also knew they came with the territory.

One time, we were in a small town in Illinois, near the end of a long, weary, difficult multi-city tour. We were tired and anxious to return home.

Earl had given an excellent talk this particular evening and we were standing backstage, meeting the audience, as was his custom.

Our host warned us that security was watching the suspicious behavior of a man who had caught their attention. The man had come backstage and was standing close enough to listen to Earl chatting with audience members. But he never moved to meet us. Soon, our host stood between him and Earl for protection.

Finally, when everyone had left, the man came over and glaring at me, hissed through clenched teeth, "I hope you know how lucky you are!"

I smiled and nodded. Our host said we needed to be going and ushered us out.

The next morning, we were getting ready to leave for the airport and Earl suggested that we stop in the coffee shop and have a bite first. We found a table in the back where it was quiet.

Soon after we ordered, the scary man from the previous evening came over to our table. He thanked Earl for his message the night before.

Then he turned to me with a look of great contempt. He told me how grateful I should be to be married to Earl. Earl interrupted and said we were both blessed to have found each other; and we were mutually grateful, all the time. The man didn't want to hear him. Again he repeated his statement.

I looked up and said, "Yes, yes I am grateful. Earl is a wonderful husband and a fun companion and we have a great marriage."

"That's not what I mean," he said, loudly. "If it weren't for this man, where would you be in this world? You'd be nowhere. You are nothing! If it weren't for this man you'd never have this kind of life."

Well, as I've pointed out before, I'm not a morning person. And I really hate having the day start on an angry or aggressive tone. Not thinking, I jumped to my feet.

"Do you see these legs?" I asked. "Do you see these feet? Well, before I met Earl, anytime I felt like going anywhere I just took myself to the airport, bought myself a ticket and went, all by myself.

"I've bought my own homes, cars, raised three children and never felt like I've missed a thing. You know nothing about me. But you are right about one thing: Earl and I are lucky to have each other.

"Any other rewards that come from being his wife, you can have – including coming to this town; because I would never have met you!" Our host, who had just come in, led the man away.

Later on the plane, we realized that he could have been that one in a million who decides to find fame through assassination.

We tried to avoid people who seemed like trouble from then on. I learned not to respond to bad situations and kept my mouth shut – most of the time.

As for the rest of the fans, we've met thousands of people I wish I had time to get to know on a personal level. And I am blessed to have been able to keep in touch with some of them. I know that even those who are irritating are just excited to meet someone famous and contract foot-in-mouth disease. They wouldn't intentionally hurt any one by being rude or unkind.

Earl used to say it wasn't important what people said or did. And he insisted that I not read newspaper interviews because, he said, reporters get caught up in what they write and make the story "better" by adding or deleting information.

I was concerned that only the truth was printed. Earl argued that as long as we knew what was true, it didn't matter what others said or believed. So he never read any of their stories. We'd still squabble when I read something inaccurate. But, he reminded me it wasn't important, as long as we knew the facts. He insisted that he was older, had been in this longer. I had to trust that he was right.

A few weeks later, we were having breakfast at a local pancake house. We were talking and laughing when a woman came over to our booth. "Oh, Mr. Nightingale, I heard you talking and just knew it had to be you. And this must be your daughter."

Earl said, "Hello. Yes, I'm Earl Nightingale, nice to meet you. This is my wife, Diana."

"Oh, well, I was sure it must be your daughter. I read somewhere that you and your daughter are very close and that she writes all of your scripts."

"Oh really? Well, that's not so. I write all of my own stuff. Always have," Earl offered defensively.

"That isn't what the article said."

Earl was turning bright red. "Ridiculous!" he boomed. "My daughter lives clear across the country. We rarely see each other. And no one has ever written anything for me. I research my own stuff and write everything myself."

"Well, that's not what I read," she said with a patient smile.

"Well, I'm telling you the truth. I do my own work."

"Yes, well, I know what I read. Nice meeting you, goodbye."

Earl was livid. Personally, I enjoyed every minute of it. The shoe on the other foot wasn't so comfortable for my sweetheart.

I patted his knee and said softly, "It doesn't matter what others think, Dear, as long as we know the truth." He knew I was teasing; but he was miserable the rest of the day.

Most of the time, even during stressful times and busy times, our sense of humor would come to our rescue. Overall, our marriage was pure fun. And our deep love for each other kept us balanced and in full awareness of what was most important to us.

Fortunately, love was something that we had in abundance. We stockpiled love. We spoke of our love for each other and demonstrated it at every opportunity.

Love wore many faces: it was the juice upon awakening or the reassurance at night after a bad dream. It was holding hands *always*, and for sure when we flew as we took off and landed – just in case.

Love prompted us to stop work to be together for lunch or to ventilate our irritations about situations out of our control. Love got us up in middle of the night to check on one another. Our love made us greater together than we were alone.

We adored one another and spent days, years collectively, challenging the writings, thoughts and philosophies of all the great minds as we played mental games with each other. He would add a thought, then I would add a thought; developing new pictures around old ideas, and asking "what if..." questions.

We wrote books together, created audio programs, influenced audiences around the world and inspired people we met. Most of all, we inspired and encouraged each other. Earl was never too busy to stop and listen to what was on my mind. Even if we were in opposition, he listened and saw my point of view. If I was too serious, he'd give me a solution with a humorous twist. I'd burst out laughing and bounce back to normal.

One day, I was going through a particularly stressful time. My domestic, personal and social responsibilities required more from me than I had time to give. It was morning and I was rushing to a meeting. Earl came in the bathroom and announced that he was out of clean underwear. Was I going to have time to do laundry that day?

It was one of those times when the final straw is placed at exactly the wrong moment, and I lost it. I wanted to know why any dirty dishes left in the sink were automatically mine, even when I left a clean kitchen in the morning and it was he who put them there at lunch time. I needed to know to whom I was suppose to report when I ran out of clean underwear and pantyhose. Where was my wife, my mother, my helper? To say I was a little upset would be an understatement. I left the house unhappy.

When I returned home that afternoon, I found a newly-written story waiting for me. Earl had composed a tale about the shipping industry.

It recalled that during the 1800s, great ships were built to haul goods from place to place. These ships were huge and would be stuffed with cargo.

More often than not, they would sink from the weight of their freight. That is, until Samuel Plimsoll, a reformer and member of the British Parliament, stepped in.

Today, there is a line painted on the hull of ships, to show the limit to which the ship may be submerged by loading. It's called the Plimsoll line.

Earl's story said each of us is like a great vessel, capable of carrying great loads and performing great tasks. But unlike a ship, we don't have a visible line to show others when we are carrying too much. We are the only ones who can determine what we can safely carry without sinking beneath our load. Therefore, we must learn to draw our own personal Plimsoll line and not allow anyone to place too much of a burden on us.

He concluded by saying no one had ever expected him to be in charge of dirty dishes and dirty underwear. And if they had, he wouldn't have liked it any more than I did.

From that day forward, he asked if I had time — or if I would mind fitting a chore into my schedule. From then on, we shared tasks. And he never had to ask me to wash his undies. I made sure he never ran out.

His attempt to understand my position always ended up in a win-win situation. I guess that's what love is all about.

Yes, we were soul mates and the journey together was joyful; not troublefree, but a joy all the same.

Chapter 9

He who bends to himself a joy
Doth the winged life destroy;
But he who kisses the joy as it flies
Lives in Eternity's sunrise.
                    Robert Blake

Laughter was the glue that kept us together when Earl and I got frayed around the edges from long hours, plane rides and life in general. No matter how tired or short-tempered we were with the rest of the world, we could always somehow manage to see the humor in what was happening around us. And we'd put our heads together and laugh. Time after time...

A few months after we were married, Earl and I drove from our home in Carmel to Medford, Oregon. We made several stops along the way, enjoying all the beautiful sights. We checked into a hotel early each afternoon, investigated the surrounding area, took a nap, ate dinner, watched a little television and retired early, so we could get an early start the next morning.

The day we left home, I wore a brand new pair of jeans and a terrific new flannel shirt. We stopped early and decided to have a nap before venturing into town to see the sights and find a restaurant.

We undressed and got into bed. Being newlyweds, nap time included lots of hugging and kissing and all that good stuff. I was enjoying my husband's advances when all of a sudden, Earl burst into fits of laughter.

I was unnerved. "What are you laughing at?" I demanded.

Every time he tried to tell me he laughed even harder. I was not the least bit amused.

Finally, between uncontrollable fits of hysteria, he gasped, "Honey, I'm really impressed!

"I've made love to my share of women. But I have to tell you, I've never made love to one who's been inspected and stamped before!"

He reached over and peeled a little round sticker with a number on it from my body. It obviously had come from my lovely new shirt! Earl teased me about that for years.

I always countered with a reminder of a honeymoon incident in San Francisco. One particularly romantic evening, Earl and I were at the Top of the Mark having a drink and watching the city as the sun set. The fog had not rolled in yet and the lights of the city coming on were beautiful.

From our table by the window, we could see forever and were fully appreciating the moment, as we sipped our drinks. The band started to play *I Left My Heart in San Francisco*. Earl smiled and leaned farther across the little round pedestal table to take my hand in his. As he leaned on the little pedestal chair, it slid from beneath him and dumped him onto the floor.

There he was, all dressed up in this very posh setting on his hands and knees. The waiter rushed over and asked what he could do to help.

I looked down at Earl there on all-fours, then up at the waiter and said, "I've never seen this man before in my life. Would you kindly remove him?"

Earl laughed so hard, I didn't think he'd ever recover enough to get up. The waiter and I were trying to help Earl up, but now we were all tickled, which affected our dexterity.

Earl was a good sport. He never missed a chance to laugh at himself.

Another time we were traveling and remembered late one night that one of Earl's quotes was supposed to be published in that month's Reader's Digest. We picked up a copy at the hotel gift shop. Once we were settled in bed, I began leafing through the pages, searching for Earl's quote.

As I flipped through the pages, I began reading all the little quotes at the bottom of the other pages and for some reason that night, they all struck us as very funny. We were so tired, the quotes seemed to have secret messages that tickled us to no end. We were having such a great time, the people in the next room pounded on the wall and screamed at us to shut up! That was funny, too. We pulled the covers up over our heads and buried our faces in our pillows.

Years later, after we had moved to Arizona, Earl managed to top his performance at the Top of the Mark. There was a cat burglar in our neighborhood. We were on the alert. Every night, Earl would inspect all the windows and doors, then lock our bedroom door and set our house alarm. He said that all good soldiers have plans for what to do in case of an attack. He outlined ours.

"If anyone ever breaks into our home," he instructed, "you make sure the door is locked. Then, call 911 while I get the shotgun. We'll wait for the police to come. But, if anyone comes through the door, I'll blast him."

I never worried about burglars and never imagined that we'd ever need this plan. But I felt good, knowing we had one just the same.

Earl would often awaken in the middle of the night with a great idea or just an urge to write. He'd get up, make coffee, go into his study and work. After a while, he'd take his coffee and go out on the terrace. I'd be jolted out of bed by the screaming alarm.

Moments later, the bedroom door would open, and Earl would sheepishly peek through the door and apologize. He frequently got up early and worked in his office. Then, he'd take a shower, open the bathroom window — and trip the alarm. So, it was almost commonplace to be rudely awakened by the annoying whine of the alarm.

Near daybreak one stormy night, the alarm went off. Again. I wondered where Earl was this time. I rolled over, so I'd be poised to hear his excuse — and he was rolling over, wondering where I'd gone.

We panicked.

"Someone tripped the alarm! Check the door," he shouted, jumping out of bed.

I raced to the bedroom door, my heart pounding. It was locked. Earl disappeared into the closet and returned with his shotgun.

"Get down behind the bed," he whispered, pointing toward the floor.

I headed that way. But, before crouching on floor, I reached inside the drawer of my nightstand, where I had stashed my .22. I checked to be sure it was loaded and ready.

"Funny, the alarm company hasn't called to see what's wrong," I said. "They always call us immediately."

"You'd better give them a ring," he suggested.

I picked up the phone. It was dead. "I'm really scared now." I said a silent prayer. "I hope the police come soon."

"*Real* soon," Earl whispered, "because I have another problem. I've got to go to the john. Keep me covered."

I nodded, feeling like Penny in a Sky King adventure. My eyes darted around the room; my index finger, on the trigger.

After a few moments, Earl returned and resumed his position next to me. "Don't be afraid, Honey. If anyone comes through that door, I'll take him out in one shot."

"You mean you're going to kill whoever comes through that door?" I asked in amazement.

"Damn right," Earl said confidently.

"Do you have any idea the mess that'll make all over this white room!?" I asked, forgetting to lower my voice. I hoped I hadn't broadcast our location to the burglar.

Earl obviously had the same concern. "The guy could be on drugs. And if he's in our house, he's going to die."

It may have been the stress of the moment, but suddenly Earl *was* Sky King!

After what seemed forever, the police appeared.

Finally, one of them spotted something. The wind had blown open an unlocked door. The same invisible culprit also had taken out a transformer down the mountain. All the phones in our area were dead.

A bit embarrassed, we thanked our police department, locked up the house good and tight this time. We put away our weapons and settled back in bed with milk and graham crackers.

Comfy and secure, we relived the scene in our minds. Now we were laughing.

The thought of me covering Earl while he went to the john! And Earl, naked, hiding next to the bed with that shotgun was far funnier than the night at the Top Of The Mark. We laughed until our sides hurt.

We were still giggling in the dark like two kids, when Earl remembered another funny story.

Years earlier, when he was young and playing Sky King – for money, not my amusement — he and a couple of his friends often went to a sleepy little campground in Michigan to fish.

Their routine was to arrive late in the afternoon, check into the small motel then go across the road to a bar, where the locals hung out. "Sky King's" visits to the motel and lake were a big hit and everyone looked forward to his return.

One afternoon after a few drinks, Earl decided to go to his room and take a nap. They didn't have air conditioning then and it was very hot. So he stripped down, lay across the bed and fell asleep.

One of Earl's buddies came in later to pick up something he'd left in the room. When he saw Earl asleep in the buff, it gave him a great idea. He ran back to the bar and told the folks that for a dollar they could come and see Sky King naked!

The story goes that everyone paid a dollar; and, with drinks in hand, walked in a procession across the road, into his motel room. They all stood around the bed, took a long look, then asked for their money back.

They say laughter is healing. If that's true, Earl and I healed each other, time and time again...

On our first trip to Hawaii, we rented a condo just a few blocks from Waikiki Beach. It was small, but we loved it. We were out and about most of the time, so the size didn't really matter.

We opened the windows and balcony doors when we arrived and never closed them the entire time we were there. Each morning, white doves would fly through the window and walk around our room. We fed them from time to time and thought it was neat that we were visited by such lovely creatures each morning.

We'd been there maybe three days, enjoying the island and spending lots of time at the beach. This particular day, we were tired and decided to return for a nap.

Once there, I decided to give myself a facial. The mask felt so cool and refreshing.

"How'd you like to have a facial?" I offered.

"If I don't have to get up or move, it sounds great." Earl mumbled.

I gathered my lotions and potions, duplicated the procedure on his face, then smeared on the mask. "Now all we have to do is lie here and relax," I sighed.

We were lying on the bed with our arms and legs wound around each other, close to sleep. "This reminds me of a play I saw years ago in Ohio," I remarked. "Arte Johnson starred in it. I remember one scene where he and his wife go to the store to buy a new bed. She wants twin beds. He doesn't.

"She goes off with the salesman to look. And he sits down on the double bed with a woman customer and tells her his side of the story. He says twin beds are unnatural, that all animals sleep together and derive great pleasure from being close. For example, he tells her, kittens and puppies sleep all wound around each other. Each time one moves, they all move.

"It was a neat play and that scene reminds me of us now." My voice was quiet, as I neared sleep.

"I saw Arte in a play once, too, but I don't remember the name," Earl responded in a hushed tone.

"*I Can't Hear You When the Water's Running,*" I replied.

Now, in a louder voice, Earl said, "I saw Arte in a play once, too. But I don't remember the name."

"That *was* the name of the play," I said in disbelief.

"Oh, I wondered why you couldn't hear me – especially since there isn't even any water running."

We burst into gales of laughter. We cracked our masks, instantly turning ourselves into decrepit-looking ceramic puppets. Every time we looked at each other, we laughed even harder.

For hours, every time we'd think about the incident, we'd collapse in uncontrollable fits of laughter. I believe if there was more laughter in marriage, there would be less heartbreak. It certainly was a vital and joyful component in our lives.

Another evening during that vacation, we flipped on the television while dressing for dinner. We discovered that the Academy Awards show was coming on. We scrapped our plans to eat out and decided to camp in front of the TV.

Earl went up to the rooftop snack bar and brought back dinner – tuna and egg salad sandwiches and candy bars for dessert. Yum. Behaving like kids every once in a while added to our pleasure, too.

Then, there were times we had to face things like grown-ups...

During that same trip, Earl took me out to the USS Arizona Memorial. Earl had been aboard the Arizona the morning it was attacked and was one of only twelve Marines who survived.

Because it was Sunday, many men were ashore when the ship was attacked. Earl lived through the devastation. But the memory of his shipmates, his buddies, burned at their stations was a nightmare that lived with him always.

Earl loved to tell me stories about living in Hawaii as a young Marine and all the mischief he and the other young men got into.

He'd tell me their names and describe them in detail — along with some of their wild escapades. Earl could really tell a story and make it live. So it was easy for me to picture these guys. I felt as if I knew every one of his shipmates personally.

Earl had returned to the memorial once before, with his son. It had been very traumatic for him. Now, he wanted to return with me. I was deeply concerned for him.

We were given a VIP excursion around the Harbor, as the entire attack on Pearl was relived for us by our sailor guide. As we approached the memorial, I became more anxious for Earl and watched him closely. But, as we stepped aboard, I was relieved to see that he was alright. I relaxed.

As we stood before the wall inscribed with the names of those still entombed below in the USS Arizona, I had the feeling that all of them, those men I had heard so much about, were there with us. They had come to meet Earl's girl.

I could see their faces, hear their laughter. Suddenly, I was overcome with grief and pain. Earl helped me to the excursion boat. I did not, could not, speak for three hours after we left.

But there were happier memories of Hawaii, too. Years later, we were there, dancing to our old favorite, *I Left My Heart in San Francisco*. Earl twirled me around, looked at me and with a serious voice said, "You know, Honey, it's like I told you on our wedding day, we may not have a long time together so let's make up for length in width. Let's celebrate our twenty-fifth anniversary tonight, just in case. If we make it, we'll do it again."

So, we celebrated our twenty-fifth anniversary that night. I'm glad we did.

Chapter 10

How sweet the moonlight sleeps upon this bank!
Here will we sit and let the sounds of music
Creep in our ears: soft stillness, and the night
Becomes the touches of sweet harmony.
                        William Shakespeare (1597)

In 1983, a seminar promoter invited Earl and me to South Africa for a speaking tour. Earl's radio program, *Our Changing World*, had been heard over Springbok Radio for many, many years.

His shows were carefully selected for overseas syndication. Those that focused on purely American issues such as the automobile industry or the corn harvest in Iowa were filtered out. Those that dealt with human behavior, personal growth, value systems, hope, faith and the like; generic shows with universal appeal, were sent overseas.

Earl's program was popular among both black and white South Africans. He had been there once before, and quickly accepted the invitation to return so he could share the beautiful country with me. He took great pleasure in my first-time experiences.

I was very excited about going. Everything and anything pertaining to it was exciting to me. I had never been farther than Hawaii. And now, I would have a chance to use my passport for the first time. I would have been excited about going anywhere that far from home. But, because Earl had told me of the beauty of the country and the people who lived there, I wanted to experience for myself this country of great controversy.

As a child, I was unaware of the injustices, racial discrimination and lynchings that were rampant in parts of my own country. As an adult, I wanted to be personally involved in the struggle for equality.

An independent thinker, I wanted to see South Africa for myself; talk to people there, from all walks of life, and find my own truth about apartheid. I anxiously prepared for the trip.

It was going to be a long tour. Our speaking schedule would take us from our home in Carmel to New Orleans and Florida. Then onto New York for a few days after we returned from South Africa. Finally, there was a venue in Billings, Montana. A long trip and lots of experiences ahead.

I wanted to document everything I encountered in South Africa. And I was afraid that fatigue and jet lag would interfere with my memory process. I didn't do much writing in those days. So I decided to take along a tape recorder, to report our daily activities. Just a few words each night, I thought, would jog our memories for later recall.

We bought an inexpensive tape recorder at K-Mart and decided to try it out to see if it worked. There we were, a man who'd been in radio for forty years, with his recording engineer/wife, playing with a thirty-nine dollar tape recorder like a couple of little kids.

We recorded memories of our fishing trip that day in the Gulf; the tiny fish we'd caught and prepared for breakfast. We remarked about how great they tasted.

Our test run sounded like an early radio program: lots of talk and very little content. Earl always wanted us to do a radio show together; and, considering that we were such hams, it probably would have been enjoyable for the listeners, as well as ourselves.

We took turns playing straight man for each other. I don't know if the rest of the world would have found much humor in what we did and said during our first foray into "documentary". But we sure had a good time doing it.

We vowed to be faithful with our reporting every day; no matter how tired we might be. We were off to a great start.

By the time we got to New Orleans, we were really into the swing of it. We recorded the sounds of Bourbon Street as we walked from club to club. Another evening, we captured Al Hirt and the sounds of the river boat as we left the dock. Its great deep horn reverberated off of the buildings.

One day while we were there, we received a call from a man I'll call Jack. He was a fan of Earl's.

Jack had visited us in Carmel. The three of us had driven down the coast for lunch. We'd spent four hours or so together.

Imagine our dismay when we returned and discovered that Jack's wife had made the trip from New Orleans with him. He had left the poor woman sitting in the car while he visited with us!

Jack knew we were in New Orleans and contacted us at our hotel. He asked to spend some time with us. Our schedule was pretty tight; but we managed to squeeze in lunch with him. We found it difficult to participate in the conversation and were happy when it was over. We vowed not to subject ourselves to him ever again.

The next day, we received a package of important papers Earl needed to sign and return to Chicago immediately. We were trying to get the package to the New Orleans airport when Jack called again. He wanted to see us just once more before we left.

I had suggested hiring a messenger to take the package to the airport. But Earl said, "Listen, we can kill two birds with one stone. We can have lunch with Jack, which will make him happy. Then, we'll have him take us to the airport on the way back. It won't be so bad, if we have a mission."

It was raining in torrents when Jack picked us up. I jumped into the back seat. I had barely sat, when I realized it was still raining on me. His roof was full of holes! Jack made no apology for the leaks. As a matter of fact, he never mentioned them at all, even though Earl and I were busy diverting the incoming water and mopping our heads.

"Look over there," he pointed, ignoring our discomfort. "That's our big cemetery. We bury our dead above the ground here, you know, because of the levees."

"Yes, Earl pointed that out to me when we came in from the airport," I replied dryly.

"You ought to do a tour and really see it up close."

"Thank you, but I really don't care to do that," I said.

"I have a friend that does tours," he continued. "I'll call her and tell her to come and pick you up at the hotel."

"Really, I don't want to go," I said, sternly.

"You really should see it," he insisted. It's different from anything you'll see anywhere else. I'll just call her when we get back and make the arrangements."

"Jack, I'm not going. I have no interest. Please, don't call her," I seethed.

Earl had been unusually silent. I glanced at him through the rear view mirror. I spotted a little gleam in his eye. He obviously was enjoying a joke of some kind, while I was growing more and more impatient with this man, riding in the back seat, soaking wet.

Jack started to say something else and Earl quietly spoke, "Diana and I don't care for the archaic ceremony of burying the dead," he said. "We much prefer the ceremony that is being practiced now in California."

I wondered what he was talking about.

"Oh?" asked Jack.

"Yeah, California is where all new ideas begin. A real bellwether state. All free-thinking people go west, because that's where all the new and exciting ideas begin." Earl was deadpan.

Earl was a master at putting people in their places with humor and I knew that Jack was about to be put in his.

"You see, we have it all figured out, to the best interest of everyone, including our ecology. Ecology is a *big* issue in California. We figure it has to start somewhere. If we don't do something about the mess we've gotten our world into, well, it just probably won't get done."

Jack was all ears and Earl was talking slowly, deliberately, in that great sincere voice.

"What happens is this. The mourners and family gather at a particularly beautiful spot on the beach just before sunset. They exchange words and hugs and sometimes they read poetry, play music and sing. There is a ceremony of sorts, depending on the persuasion of the dearly departed.

"They watch the sunset, which, of course, is very symbolic. Then, just as the sun slips over the horizon, the dearly departed, who has been strapped to a mini-rocket, is launched up and out into the night sky over the ocean. At exactly the precise moment when the rocket has reached its highest altitude, there is an explosion in which the dearly departed is blown to smithereens, falls into the ocean and, of course, is returned to the universe in a perfectly natural way.

"It's all very beautiful — and a much more natural way to be disposed of. Don't you agree, Jack?"

Well, Jack was duly impressed. "Great idea! I hadn't heard about it before. But great idea!"

I was frantically trying to maintain a straight face. Finally, I scooted forward to the edge of my seat, so I could hide my face in my hands on the back of the seat. I no longer thought about the rain or this boring, exasperating man. Suppressing laughter was now a full-time job as my sweet, darling husband sat smugly with a straight face, looking out through the windshield at the pouring rain.

Back in our hotel that night, we held each other and howled, as we relived the day. We captured the experience on our little tape player to be re-lived and re-laughed over the coming years.

The next day, we were off to New York's JFK airport.

After hours on the runway, we finally took off. Once we reached a safe altitude, the magnificent food service began. It was indescribable – simply the best! I was having the time of my life; saying "yes" to everything they offered me.

I even accepted several little bottles of vodka, even though I wasn't drinking it. Earl reminded me that we didn't need to be stockpiling things that were of no use to us. He called me a "pack rat" and teased me unmercifully about my little stash.

"Suppose the plane crashes and we need these for medicinal purposes?" I asked seriously. "One never knows. In today's world, one can't be too well-prepared. When I was a Girl Scout leader..."

Earl was having fun with this and getting a very big kick out of me. I never knew why Earl found so much humor in what I said; but he used to say that it was like being married to his own personal comedian. I was amazed. After all, I was usually serious.

International health laws required that the plane be sprayed for bacteria, insects and whatever. They announced that they were going to spray the cabin and suggested that perhaps we cover our faces with a handkerchief to protect ourselves.

I was asleep. So Earl, being the loving and thoughtful husband that he was, decided to cover my face for me with his handkerchief.

Earl had very large hands and incredible strength. So, when he took his folded handkerchief and placed it over my nose and mouth in my sleep, I thought I was being smothered by God only knows who or what.

Not being a sedate person, I came up fighting for my life. By the time I was fully awake and fully apprised of the situation, my darling husband was once again hysterical with laughter.

"I wish you could have seen the fight you put up," he howled.

"Yeah, well, you tried to smother me," I scowled.

"I was trying to protect you from the spray." He was serious about his intent, but chuckling all the same.

"Well, with that much pressure, you all but protected me from the rest of my life!"

He put his big arms around me and gave me a kiss.

I couldn't help laughing. But, for years, I gave him a bad time about the attempted murder onboard the jet to South Africa. And every time, he'd laugh just as loudly as he had back then.

We loved South Africa and the people with whom we came in contact. We hadn't wanted the sanitized tour of the country. And we had an opportunity to see much of it; but not nearly enough.

The promoter, Chris, had not represented himself or the tour with complete truth and accuracy. There were a number of misunderstandings between us and the tension built as the tour progressed.

One evening, Earl spoke for about an hour and a half to a full house on his prepared topic. When he was finished, Chris told us there would be a short break. Then he had scheduled an additional speech on the subject of family and child-raising.

Earl said, "You have a real problem on your hands. I'm through. You said nothing about an additional talk. I've said all I have to say. Good luck."

Chris was nervous and had every reason to be. "What will I do? I have these people coming back after the break and I promised that there would be more. It's too late to find someone else. You've got to help me out."

Earl didn't push easily, and by now was completely out of patience with Chris.

"Sounds serious, Chris. Maybe you can talk Diana into doing it. She's an expert on kids and all that. Maybe, if you ask her real nice, she'll help you out."

I wasn't anxious to bail out Chris, either. He had lied about so much that we were really feeling used. Earl refused to go back out. I felt that the audience shouldn't suffer because of Chris, and agreed to take over after the break.

Shortly, I found myself addressing my first foreign audience, enjoying the challenging questions raised by an audience completely different from those in the States.

Earl was very pleased that I took on the job with no notice and was happy with the way the evening turned out. He smiled and said, "I've just been waiting for the chance to do that. You've been in the background too long. That's where you belong – center stage." I realized for the first time that Earl had other plans for me.

The next night, Chris informed us that I would have to remain in Johannesburg the following day while he and Earl flew to Durban. We had looked forward to Durban and couldn't understand the sudden change of plans.

"Sold out. The plane is just sold out," Chris said. "Not another seat to be had."

Earl was upset. "You were supposed to have taken care of all the transportation arrangements prior to our arrival. Every day it's something new to deal with. I'll call the airline myself.

"If Diana doesn't go, neither do I. I refuse to leave her here alone. So you may have to cancel tomorrow night's talk.

"Where is it anyway? And how come it isn't on our itinerary?"

Now it was Chris' turn to be upset. After some argument, he said he'd try once again to book another seat and that he'd get back to us. In just minutes, he called all happy with, "Good news – I got a seat."

"That's good, now tell me where I'm speaking."

"It's not a big audience, just a group of businessmen. But they'd be disappointed if you didn't come." He said nothing more.

The next morning when we boarded the plane, Earl and I noticed that there were a large number of empty seats. Why had there been a problem booking one for me? We landed and were met by a representative of Earl's radio sponsor and some of the leaders of the Indian community.

They were warm, friendly and anxious to show us their city. We were taken to an Indian restaurant they had closed to the public, in our honor. They had invited several people to join us for breakfast.

There were several reminders of home. They served us a juice that looked and tasted very much like Tang. And, from the speakers, the voice of Glen Campbell, singing *Wichita Lineman*. There we were in Durban, South Africa, in an East Indian restaurant listening to country/western music. I was amused.

One of the men sitting with us asked me why I was smiling. I told him I hadn't expected to hear Glen Campbell and that it was just a happy response.

He said they had wanted to make us feel at home. But, he added, they also really liked American music.

He had another friend who owned a very fine restaurant that was open only in the evening. He asked if we'd like to have dinner there with him and some friends that night. He said the food was authentic East Indian, and so was the music.

This was what I had wanted to experience — the real South Africa; not just what our white sponsors wanted us to see. I wanted to talk with people of color who were raising their families and earning a living here.

Earl and I quickly accepted the invitation. As we were getting in the car to go to the hotel, Chris approached us. He was very angry. He told us we were not to accept invitations he didn't arrange. He didn't want us to be with anyone else. Furthermore, we didn't have time for dinner, since Earl had a meeting that night. We'd just better forget it.

Before then, I had let Earl and Chris battle it out when things turned sour. But this time, I was angry.

I tersely informed Chris that the time not spent working belonged to us, to spend anyway and with anyone we wished. I told him that I was interested in meeting people one-on-one, not just in select groups.

"I want to talk to people about real things and I want to eat their food and enjoy their music with them. You're out of line. And we *are* going."

Chris was red in the face and very upset.

Late that afternoon, we were driven to the restaurant, where we were joined by several people. We laughed and exchanged stories. We were particularly amused by the placemats, which read, "Eating with utensils is like making love with your clothes on."

The music was beautiful and the people were like old friends.

One of the men in our party that evening had come from Johannesburg to hear Earl speak. He suggested that I might enjoy going to the flea market in the Indian part of town when I got back. He said I would enjoy the experience.

I agreed that it sounded like a good idea.

We were enjoying coffee after dinner when a driver appeared at our table.

"Mr. Nightingale, Mrs. Nightingale, I've come to fetch you."

"It's early, isn't it? The meeting isn't for hours." Earl looked at Chris. Chris's face was red again and he looked uncomfortable.

"I've come to take Mrs. Nightingale to the hotel before taking you to the club, Sir."

"Diana's coming with me. What club? What's going on here anyway?" Now Earl was glaring at Chris. Chris was silent.

"What's going on?" Earl insisted.

"Surely, Sir, you understand – I mean about the club and all."

"What club? I don't know anything other than I have a talk to give this evening to some businessmen."

"Well, Sir, you have been invited to speak to the Circle Century Club. It's very old and you have to be very special to be invited – like Winston Churchill who once came. And well, it's very exclusive. It's a – men's club." His eyes were on me now.

There was silence. Earl looked at Chris and said, "I'm not going. You tried to pull another fast one on us. I'm through!"

Diana — 1 year old

(above): Diana

Diana — 5 years old

Diana's Father and Mother

Diana — 7 years old

Diana — 13 years old

Diana — 18 years old

Earl, Don & Bert
(Brothers)

Earl's brother,
Bert, and Earl at 3 years old

Earl
Placerville, CA

Earl's Mother,
Honey (Gladys) at 16

Earl — U.S. Marine Corp., Pearl Harbor

Sky King Radio Show Characters
Top, black hat – Clipper (nephew) — Center – Penny (niece)
Bottom left, checkered shirt – Jim Bell, ranch foreman
Bottom right, white tie — Earl as Sky King

Earl and Queen Elizabeth

Wedding Day
left to right: Lloyd Conant, Earl & Diana, Hazel Conant

Diana & Earl
on a cruise

Earl & Diana
in Arizona

Earl & Diana — Carmel, CA

Diana & Earl in Alaska

Earl & Diana in Alaska
(Christmas Card)

Earl & Diana, Lake Powell, AZ

Diana & Earl

Earl & Diana, South Africa

Children (left to right) – Kim, Dayne and Jill

Children (left to right) – Dayne, Kim and Jill

Granddaughter, Sabra

Grandchildren, Juliette and Jordan

Mother and Diana

Diana and Noya in Berlin

Diana — Australia, in chopper

Grandson Dan in Alaska

Diana in Naples

"Chris," I said, "Why the secrecy? This is what the plane ticket fiasco was all about isn't it? How dare you place us in this situation."

"I'm not going anywhere except back to the hotel," Earl interrupted.

"But the men are waiting..." Chris protested.

"You should have thought of that sooner," Earl told him. "Did you really think that once we were here you could just manipulate us at will?"

Things were heating up and I was furious. The driver was shuffling, trying to find an acceptable compromise.

Earl wouldn't budge. If I couldn't go with him, he wasn't going. Chris kept saying that I wasn't "allowed," and we should be reasonable. The driver was most concerned about the "members" who were anticipating his return with Earl Nightingale.

Finally, I asked if there might be an area that was not part of the club, a room or an office perhaps where I might read and wait.

Yes, there was a bar and one could entertain guests there, I was told. Even women were permitted on occasion.

That was fine with me. It was not fine with Earl, however. After much discussion, the driver said he knew that once the members were informed of the mix up, they would make an exception and I could be a guest as well.

Earl said if that were the case, he'd go. So off we went in silence to "the club." We were met at the entrance and Earl was greeted most warmly. I stepped up close to Earl and whispered, "I'll be waiting for you in the bar."

He had no time to argue, as he was escorted into the club. I was taken to the bar. It was a lovely room. The driver turned out to be a member. He graciously stayed with me during Earl's talk.

After the meeting, most of the men wanted an opportunity to speak to Earl and lingered in the meeting room for a while. Apparently, Earl had explained the confusion; and when the others came into the bar, they came over and greeted me.

They hoped that I wasn't unhappy and that I'd been comfortable. They assured me that I really would have been welcome to join the meeting.

I explained that I had a delightful evening and had no desire to break anyone's tradition. What I didn't say was I had been experiencing discrimination ever since the driver appeared at the restaurant. And, I didn't like it.

I told them I had too much pride to have anyone make allowances for me; that I went first class, or not at all. Well, these dyed-in-the-wool traditionalist South African gentlemen thought I was great — a woman who knew her place! I clearly had charmed them.

The president of the club took my hand. Turning to Earl, he said, "You must let us know in advance when you plan to return to South Africa. Next time, we will invite Diana to be our guest speaker and you will have to wait in the bar." We all laughed.

As the evening progressed, I sensed that they were beginning to admit how unreasonable and insensitive it was to cling to their exclusionary rules — in this instance, and others. Perhaps Earl's message had gotten through.

We visited Cape Town. Then, it was back to Johannesburg. We had reservations on the famous Blue Train. Earl had loved trains all of his life, this being the far extreme from when he had hopped on with the hobos, as a poor teenager.

Later, he traveled across the states by train and loved sleeping on them. Riding on the Blue Train was a dream come true.

We had a lovely compartment with a bathroom. I was looking out the window when I noticed there was a little knob on the wall that indicated music and radio. I turned it on and I couldn't believe my ears. They were broadcasting Earl's *Our Changing World* over Springbok radio!

We listened to his program as we dressed for dinner, then went into the bar to wait for our table. The bartender looked amazed when he heard Earl's voice ordering a drink. "I can't believe it's really you!"

He went over to a drawer and pulled out a menu. "Will you autograph this menu please?"

Earl smiled and started signing it.

"This is great! You know, my two favorite people in the whole world have sat right here at my bar. Now I have both of their autographs on the same menu. Wow! Earl Nightingale and Elton John."

Earl leaned over to me and whispered, "Who's Elton John?"

Later, when we returned to Johannesburg, we visited our friends, Terry and Noya. Earl had met them during his first speaking tour years before. They had remained good friends and visited us whenever they were in the States.

Terry was head of the Dale Carnegie Training Schools. Noya was a professor who taught Hebrew Literature at the university. We didn't see them often; but felt close to them, like family. We cherished our time together.

Time was slipping by; and I really wanted to go to the flea market suggested to me. Earl was tied up with his sponsor that Saturday morning. So I decided to grab a cab and go alone.

I barely had seated myself in the back seat, when I noticed that the cab driver had a distinctly hostile attitude toward me. I had only asked him to take me to the flea market. So I wasn't sure what his problem was.

He immediately drew my attention to the vans, parked along the street. There were lots of them, to be sure. But I hadn't noticed them before. He asked me if I knew what they were for.

"Transportation, would be my guess," I said, smiling.

"The government proides them for the blacks!" he snapped. "We have to worry about our own transportation. And *they* get picked up! You have no idea how the government coddles them!"

I tried changing the subject. "Where are you from?"

"I'm an Afrikaner!" he shouted. "This is *our country!*"

He then went into a tirade about the blacks; outlining the social injustices that were being perpetrated against the Afrikaners. It was quite amazing to listen to this man's twisted beliefs. It was even more amazing when he turned his attack toward people like me who supported "those others" by going to places like their flea market.

Well, there it was; the reason he was so upset with me from the start.

As we pulled up to the curb of the flea market, I reached into my pocket for the fare.

As I handed it to him, I said, "Well, it's been most interesting to hear your opinion on what's wrong with the government, the blacks, the colored — and people like me.

"But one thought has been playing over and over again in my mind. If you were so fortunate to be born a superior white male, with all the unlimited opportunities it gives you, why in the world didn't you do something with your life? Why are you driving a cab?"

I was out of the cab by now.

"When it comes time to leave here," he yelled, "no one's going to come and pick you up! You'll have plenty of time to get to know these people!" he threatened.

I briskly walked to the first stall and was greeted by a smiling face.

I stayed until the flea market closed, buying souvenirs and talking with the people. When it was time to go, a man at one of the stands called a cab for me. The ride back to the hotel was much more pleasant.

The speaking tour finally ended and we had earned our time alone. We had reservations at Kirkman's Camp, a small camp out in the transvaal. Seeing the wild animals in their natural surroundings was almost more than a city girl could hope for.

We flew by small plane to Nelspruit where we were met by a driver who had been sent by the camp. We had driven for about an hour and a half when he pulled the van into a lovely hotel for tea. Being a tea drinker, I loved the idea of stopping for tea.

In the States, we tea drinkers are a nuisance. Overseas, we are "civilized."

After a short rest, we resumed our trip, winding along dirt roads past the homelands, seeing women with children strapped to their backs, washing clothes in the streams and river.

It seemed strange to look out the window of the van and see zebras, impalas and giraffes grazing and eating leaves off the trees. We arrived at camp just at sundown. We were received and, as we were being shown to our small, modest cabin, told that only the kitchen staff was on site because everyone else was out for the evening "watch."

It was suggested that we clean up, then come to the main building for refreshments and wait for the others to return for dinner.

"Refreshments" sounded good to Earl. It had been a long, dusty, tiring trip.

"I just want to get this dirt off of my body and have a nice cold martini," Earl said wearily.

We cleaned up and walked out into the night air. It was magical. We found comfortable chairs on the veranda.

A young man came up to us, bowed and asked what we would like to have.

"Vodka martini, please," Earl said.

"We don't have that, sir."

"Well, just vodka then."

"No, sir. We have only beer and wine. No vodka."

"What do you mean — 'no vodka'?"

"Sorry, sir. Only beer and wine."

"I'll have wine, please," I said.

"Nothing for me," Earl said. He sounded tired and disappointed. He had worked hard. All he wanted was a vodka.

I excused myself, saying that I forgotten something and returned to our cabin. I rifled through my baggage, now several weeks familiar. I knew where everything was. Everything had its place. That way, I didn't have to pack and unpack every time we moved.

I felt around the upper right-hand corner of my carry-on bag until I found what I was searching for, picked them up and placed them in my sweatshirt pocket. I grabbed a glass from the night stand and returned to the side of my sad companion.

"Hi, sailor! Care for a drink?" I held out a glass and two small bottles of vodka from the plane. Earl's face lit up.

"You beautiful, wonderful person! If we weren't married already, I'd ask you now and wouldn't take no for an answer. I'm married to a pack rat and I love it! I love you! You'll never get away from me."

My wine arrived and we toasted to "us" as we always did. We sat there, alone in this strange camp, staring up into the pitch black sky at stars that were so bright, so big and so dense that we were silenced by the splendor of it all.

In the distance, we could hear the hyenas calling to one another in the jungle. Soon, we became aware of the sky turning brighter to the right of us and, as we watched, the moon began to climb up into the jungle sky. It was full, and not just orange but appeared to be molten gold, huge and breathtaking. And no one was there but the two of us. We knew it was just for us.

"Thanks, God," we said aloud. We held hands and sipped our drinks.

We recorded our entire trip and ended up with ten sides of dialogue that today are priceless to me. I hear us talk about the day's events, sometimes with tired voices that are almost asleep. Then Earl will say, "Anything else, Angel?"

"No, I don't think so."

"Okay, that's it then, 'til tomorrow. Good night, darling, I love you."

"I love you, too."

Now, on nights when there's a big, orange, full moon, I listen to those tapes, remember and live it all over again. And, like the illusion of radio, I imagine that we are alive and well, together and happy in democratic South Africa.

Chapter 11

A book of verses underneath the bough,
A jug of wine, a loaf of bread – and thou
Beside me singing in the wilderness –
Oh wilderness were Paradise now.
                    Edward Fitzgerald (1857)

During our first year together, Earl and I shared all the happy and sad stories about our lives before we met. I told Earl the story about the balloon man and Earl shared with me his childhood memories.

Earl would go on for hours about his life as a child and how hard times had been during the Great Depression. If times weren't bad enough, his father was a drifter who was always coming up with new money-making ideas, like pear farming in northern California. To fulfill his dreams, the family moved often.

Earl remembered when he and his brothers were quite small, they had a pet pig they called Squeegee. Squeegee followed them everywhere they went, running as fast as her short little legs would take her.

On school mornings, they would have to out-run her, so she would stay home. At the end of the day, Squeegee would squeal happily as she ran to meet them. They loved her dearly. She was more fun than any other pet they'd ever had.

One day when the boys returned home, Squeegee was nowhere to be found. They looked in all of her favorite hiding places and secret play areas, calling her name. Could it be she was lost? They looked and looked.

Suddenly they rounded the corner of their house – and out back, hanging from a tree was Squeegee. The boys became hysterical. Who could have done a thing like this to their beloved Squeegee?

Then they spied the villain. It was their father. He tried to explain to the boys he had killed Squeegee because they had no money to buy food. He had no choice, he said.

Earl and his brothers sobbed and screamed. How could their father do such a thing? They would rather starve to death themselves, than eat their beloved Squeegee – and no one did. Poor Squeegee had died in vain.

Poor Squeegee and poor Earl. Somehow my story about the balloon man paled next to Earl's sad story. After all, it was only a balloon. And my dad and I had resolved all of that before he died.

My story touched Earl's heart, though. It made him sad. In fact, it made him cry. He said he couldn't bear the thought of me not having something as simple as a balloon. He vowed that I'd never want for a "balloon" again as long as I lived. True to his promise, through the following years, on special occasions and for no special occasion, I would receive a present or surprise from Earl and he'd say, "just a little balloon."

There was something else I wanted when I was a little girl — to visit Greece one day. My father used to tell me all kinds of wonderful stories about what it was like to be a boy in Greece, running barefoot in the sand along the water's edge to school.

Daddy said one time my grandfather bought him a new pair of shoes and sternly warned him against getting them wet and ruining them in the salt water. Remembering the look on his father's face, and knowing there'd be hell to pay, my father took off his new shoes and put them behind a rock before running off to play with the other boys.

When it finally came time to leave, Dad couldn't remember where he'd left his shoes. He searched until it was too dark to see, and finally went home without them.

My father was a great story teller. Each event he told me about created mental pictures of his native island and the country he loved so much. I promised myself at an early age that one day I would visit Samos Island and see this beautiful place.

When I had dinner with Earl that first evening in Punta Gorda, I told him I was planning on going to Greece sometime in the very near future. I had a separate account into which I put all of the bonus money I earned. I called it my Greek Fund. Earl had been impressed.

During our marriage, the majority of our travel was work-related. We went on day trips and did weekend fun things. But, as a rule, we didn't take off to far away places to do things just for fun.

We had moved to Paradise Valley, Arizona. It was July, and the temperature was well over 110 degrees. (Yes, but it's a dry heat, you say. Let me tell you – go sit in a sauna, crank that baby up to 120 degrees and stay in there for a few weeks. Come back; then, and we'll talk *dry heat!*)

We had been running errands and were both so hot, our skin hurt. Earl never gave weather any consideration and that day was no different. It was, as far as he was concerned, a great day to go out to lunch.

We happily sat in the cool comfort of Houlihan's restaurant in the Biltmore shopping center, discussing the upcoming board meeting in Chicago.

"We'll go in on Tuesday, get the meeting over and come home on Friday, the fourteenth," Earl said.

"But that's my birthday!" I protested. The board meeting was always held on the same dates; and we had always celebrated my birthday in Chicago. "Why don't we stay for the weekend and come home Sunday like we have in the past?"

"Can't do that," he said, "I'll be too pressed for time before I have to leave again."

Earl never went anywhere without me. I booked all of our trips and I hadn't heard of any last minute speech scheduled for the following next week.

"Where are you going?"

"I'm leaving Tuesday for Greece. Would you like to come along and celebrate your birthday on a nice cruise of the Greek Islands — maybe find someone you know on your father's island?"

I looked at him in amazement. I couldn't believe my ears. I just sat and stared at him until the full impact of what he'd said hit me. Earl was smiling. I leaned forward, buried my face in my arms and began to sob.

"The big balloon," Earl said with pride. Tears filled his eyes, a loving smile on his face, "I hope your reaction means yes; and you'll go with me."

The big balloon indeed. At that moment, all the pain and disappointment I'd felt as a child, wanting a simple balloon and not getting one, faded away. The pure joy I felt at that moment made up for it all.

People at the tables around us stared and whispered. I suppose they thought Earl had said some horrible, hateful thing. In fact, he had just given me the greatest love gift I could ever want.

We went off to Chicago for the meeting and hurried back home. I always thought that when I got ready to go to Greece, I'd take months to make arrangements to find my father's family; lay the groundwork for the trip by writing letters and making plans.

But, with such short notice, I only had time to call my cousin, John, in Cleveland to get a few names. He told me there was a relative by marriage in Athens. But there were first cousins who lived in my father's village. If I just went there and asked around, I'd find them. It would be easy. Easy for him, I thought, he speaks Greek! I, on the other hand, was limited to English.

The flight was exciting and the fact that the airline left much to be desired did not dampen my enthusiasm one bit. We arrived in Athens in the morning, caught a cab to the Hotel Grande Bretagne, unpacked and went to bed.

When I awoke, it was early evening. I stepped out on to our little balcony to the sounds of the activities below in the square. It was music to my ears. I looked off into the distance and could see the Acropolis, lighted in all of its glory. I felt as though I had lived there a lifetime. I had truly come home.

Earl had planned for us to spend three or four days in Athens, resting from the flight and adjusting to the time difference before our cruise. It afforded us a chance to fully explore Athens, with all of her beautiful sights.

From our room at the Hotel Grande Bretagne, we not only could see the lights on the Acropolis at night, we could watch all of the evening activities in the square below. In the morning, Earl would sit by the window with his coffee and try to read the signs on the buildings across the way. They were, of course in Greek, but he was sure one of them said something about Arnold Palmer. I'd laugh, then I'd cry.

We had to go to the local travel agent to pick up our cruise materials. And as we were leaving, the agent asked if she could do anything else to help us. I told the agent I had a relative in Athens and wanted her to know I was at the hotel, even though I wasn't sure she'd be at all interested. I gave her the name.

We left, had lunch and poked around the shops. When we returned to our hotel room, the message light was flashing on our phone. My cousin wanted me to call her right away!

My heart raced as I dialed the number. Why hadn't I at least learned a few words in Greek on the plane, or brought a dictionary or something with me? What could I say to make her understand?

A young woman answered the phone. Thank God, she spoke English. She was my cousin's daughter. Within two hours, she, her boyfriend, her mother Mary, as well as another cousin arrived at the hotel. Strangers for a lifetime; now we were a family coming together with laughter, hugs and tears. It was wonderful to meet my father's family – my family, at long last.

In no time at all, we were off to see their Athens. We saw all their favorite haunts – places we would never have seen as a tourists – and wound up in a wonderful, small outdoor restaurant eating everybody's favorite, pizza. We ordered too much, as always, and had the leftovers boxed to take back to the hotel with us.

It had been a magical evening. Now we were sitting enjoying the last of our coffee. I wished aloud that I had been given just a little more time to plan, so I could have contacted everyone on Samos in advance. It would be so difficult to locate relatives now.

With questioning looks, they all began talking at once; making it difficult for Anna to interpret. "No problem," she said. She reached for our pizza box and began to write names on the top of the box. My grandparents' names were included for reference.

"How do I get there? What are their addresses?"

Blank stares. "Just go there and ask," they responded. There it was again. First, cousin John had said how easy it would be and now these folks. Maybe they all forgot I didn't speak the language. But since they made it all sound so simple, I smiled and nodded.

When Friday came, we left for our cruise of the islands. The ship was dirty. The service was non-existent; the staff, rude. But we didn't care; we were having a ball. At the end of the cruise, we flew to Samos Island for the final balloon.

Our travel agent in Scottsdale had booked us at a hotel on Samos. Never having been there herself, and not asking its location vis-a-vis my father's village, we found ourselves on the opposite side of the island from our destination.

We rented a little Suzuki open vehicle and took off for the other side, "letting the good times roll."

The island was beautiful. It was difficult to keep my eyes on the road, with so many wonderful sites to distract me. We zipped along the road without a clue, a road map or directions; only family names scribbled on top of our pizza box. We'd since eaten the pizza, of course, and had disposed of the lower portion of the box but kept the top. (I still have it!)

We found the town that was supposed to be closest to Dad's village. As soon as we arrived, we spotted a lovely hotel and went in to freshen up and have an iced tea.

It didn't take more than a few minutes to agree that we should go back to our hotel, pack a few days' worth of clothes and move to this more convenient location.

It was a silly, laughter-filled drive back around the island, singing, *On the Road Again* and other fun songs. There was literally no traffic, and I really flew; so we arrived quickly. We packed a bag and told the proprietor of our plans. He was not pleased.

He knew we'd need our passports to check into the other hotel; but was reluctant to give up his control of them. After much conversation, a few mild threats from Earl, and the request of a bribe from the proprietor, he relented and gave us our passports. With that accomplished, we were back on the road, around the island and settled in our new abode by late afternoon.

"What would you like to do now?" Earl asked.

"Are you tired?"

"Not me. I'm up to whatever your little heart desires."

I jumped to my feet. "Good, let's go find the family."

"Do you know where to go?"

"We've got our pizza box and each other. What more can we need?"

We left the coast behind and began driving up a narrow road that wound around and around, back and forth, until at last it came to a fork. One side was paved, the other wasn't.

"Now what? Which way are you going?" Earl asked.

I had been driving like a woman possessed. "I'm taking the dirt road. I just feel like that's the right way."

We left a great cloud of dust behind us, as we headed up the dirt road. It was getting late and we still had no idea where we were or where we were going. Suddenly, the road came to an abrupt end in a church parking lot.

"Now what?" Earl asked.

"This is it, I just know it. Come on." My heart was pounding. We left our little Suzuki in the church parking lot, passed through a gate and found ourselves standing in front of an old church. I tried the door. It was locked.

We walked through the courtyard and stood atop a hill that looked like every postcard I'd ever seen of Greece.

It was lovely. There were white buildings with brightly painted doors lining the spotlessly clean hillside where flowers grew in abundance in pots and window boxes. Being late in the day, it was hot and humid, but felt wonderful to my skin. Two young women sat on the curb outside the church, talking.

"Excuse me, please," I said. "Do you speak English?"

They stood up, smiled and walked toward us. "A little," they said, nodding.

After waiting a lifetime, I was finally here and couldn't wait another minute. I made no attempt to use my one Greek greeting or English social amenities. "Good, I'm looking for this woman," I blurted out, pointing to the name on the pizza box. "She's my cousin. I'm from America. My name is Diana. My father was Dimetri Giannis. This is a picture of him. He was born here. Can you help me?"

I was trying to tell the story, keep it simple and just find out if this was the place I'd hoped to find for so many years. They looked at the names, conversed back and forth and after a second or two, smiled, nodded, and shouted in unison, "Margitsa! Margitsa!"

Just a few yards down the hill, a green door swung open. Time stood still. A petite woman, dressed in black with the face of a child, stepped through the doorway and walked toward us. She greeted the girls, smiled at us, then returned her attention to the girls.

A conversation began with the girls pointing to the picture of my father, the names on the pizza box and then to me. The woman studied the names, looked at me and asked the girls something.

I pointed to the picture of my father and said, "Dimetri – my father." I was choking up.

A look of recognition and delight swept across the woman's face. She grabbed my hands and asked, "Dimetri? Elyria?"

"My father," I nodded, tears streaming down my face.

She put her arms around me. She was rocking me in her arms, talking softly in Greek, as we stood sobbing.

Earl busily handed out tissues – which was a full-time job. Every now and then we'd stop to blow our noses. Then we'd laugh, hug and start crying all over again.

Holding my arm tightly, Margitsa turned and said something to the girls, her tear-stained face beaming with joy. The girls took off down the hill as she led us to her home. It was scrubbed clean as though she had been expecting us for weeks. She served us coffee, fruit and cookies.

We sat, touching each other on the face and arms. The family resemblance between Margitsa, my sisters and me was unreal. Margitsa was my father's younger sister's daughter – my first cousin.

Meanwhile, the girls from the church had accomplished their mission. They had gone to my cousin, John's, house down the hill to announce our arrival. Soon, the entire village had been alerted. As fate would have it, a relative from Cleveland was there visiting friends and quickly offered to act as interpreter.

It was just about unbelievable that we were here at last and that it had been so easy, just as everyone had said it would be. And so perfect.

Margitsa took me by the hand and led me through the village telling everyone who I was. Many of the villagers who had been children with my father were now joining in our joyous homecoming. We walked to the remains of the building where my father had been born, and visited the sites where my grandparents and aunts had lived. I gathered up pieces of broken pottery that I found in my father's house to take home to my mother, sisters, and brother. The only thing that would have made this any more perfect would have been if they, along with my father, could have been there too.

The next few days, I shall treasure for the rest of my life; the joy of the reunion and the realization of a lifetime dream. Earl had indeed given me the balloon of balloons!

Chapter 12

Our birth is but a sleep and a forgetting;
The soul that rises with us, our life's star,
Hath had elsewhere its setting,
And cometh from afar:
Not in entire forgetfulness
And not in utter nakedness,
But trailing clouds of glory do we come
From God who is our home.
William Wordsworth (1845)

While we were in Greece, Earl noticed an old familiar feeling in his chest. He'd felt like that before he required his first heart surgery. He decided to get a thorough check up when we returned home.

Back in Phoenix, x-rays confirmed our suspicions. But the physician recommended medication before jumping into surgery.

As the months passed, it became obvious that medication was not the answer; and we began making plans to proceed with the replacement of his heart valve.

Aside from the leaky porcine valve, Earl was in such good health the surgeon chose to replace the porcine with an artificial valve that would not wear out in eight or ten years, but last a lifetime.

A few weeks before Earl entered the hospital for surgery, we sat together in our big lounger on the terrace. We were reminiscing about all the wonderful things we had done together through the years. He asked me if there were any balloons left – anything in the whole world that I still wanted. I told him not a one.

As a matter of fact, his love and devotion always reminded me of the words from the song, *Time in a Bottle:*

"If I had a box just for wishes and dreams that had never come true, the box would be empty except for the memory of how they were answered by you."

He smiled.

It was time to decide when he would be admitted to the hospital. Earl took a lot of things into consideration — not the least of which was his birthday. Cake and ice cream were favorites of his. And he loved to celebrate and receive gifts. (He was the master gift-giver, also.)

With March 12th properly celebrated, Earl entered the hospital the following Monday evening, to begin blood work and pre-op requirements.

Avoiding the seriousness of the impending surgery, we tried to keep up each other's spirits with light conversation and jokes. About eight o'clock, a man came by Earl's room to "cheer us up."

He said he was from the "zipper club", and explained that Earl would be a member of the club after his surgery. Not realizing to whom he was speaking, he advised Earl of the importance of a positive mental attitude. Earl teased, as he left, that he thought it was a "very novel idea".

I stayed with Earl until they finally threw me out, insisting that he needed to rest for his surgery the next day.

I tried sleeping, but tossed and turned without Earl there beside me. We were seldom apart. I already missed him and hoped they let him come home soon after surgery.

After a few hours, I decided to go back to the hospital and at least sit with Earl.

The hospital was quiet when I arrived. Sounds of sleeping patients could be heard from the hall. The nurses were gathered at their stations doing paperwork and chatting. I waved at them as I went by. One of them put her hands on her hips, smiled and shook her head. She knew I needed to be there.

Earl was awake and happy to see me. He had refused a sleeping pill and hadn't slept either. He scooted over and made room for me on the bed. I lay down. He put his arm around me and I rested my head on his chest.

We didn't speak for a long time; we just lay there looking out through the window at the mountain, barely visible in the predawn light. Finally, Earl spoke.

"You know Honey, I sure wish I could put you in a beautiful golden cage where you would be protected from all pain and suffering when I'm not around to protect you."

He paused. "But of course if I did that, I'd be protecting you from all the good things in the world too, and I wouldn't want that.

"I know it hasn't always been easy being married to me. You've had so much to worry about, with my health. And there's always been such a demand on you, being my wife and all."

Another pause. "But I'm worth it!" he smiled. "I'm a hell of a nice guy!"

We both burst out laughing – fighting back tears. The sun was rising now and the mountain looked like a sleeping giant in the red morning light.

Having regained my composure, I spoke. "Looks like it's going to be a beautiful day. And your heart sounds like it's working really well. How 'bout if you get dressed while I go get the car. We can go have some breakfast and go to the zoo."

That sounded good to Earl. We were snuggling and joking when the doctor came in. Seeing our happy state of mind, he reminded us that we were facing a "life-threatening situation."

I told him I'd searched all night for a fine line permanent marker. I wanted to draw directions to Earl's heart on his chest; along with a reminder to take extra good care of him and send him back to me in good health, because I loved him very much.

The doctor was neither amused nor impressed. When he left, he had succeeded in creating a more somber mood. Earl and I were keenly aware of the fact that we were, indeed, involved in a life-threatening situation.

Sitting in the waiting room, the next hours seemed to last forever. Every now and then, Earl's cardiologist would come out of the operating room to update me on the progress.

Finally, it was over. Surgery had gone exceptionally well. The cardiologist was extremely pleased that, when the surgeon completed the heart valve exchange and took Earl off of the heart machine, his heart took over nicely. It was strong and didn't miss a beat. He warned me, though, that the first 48 hours would be critical.

During the next two days, Earl progressed at an outstanding pace.

The entire surgical staff was so impressed with the way Earl responded with a positive attitude and good cheer to the many tasks that were required of him, they made him their "star patient."

As a reward, I was allowed to stay longer with him, which made us both happy. During those hours, and under those circumstances, we still found things to laugh about.

The doctor and nurses were checking the 14 computerized monitors and medication machines attached to Earl and making notations on his chart. Earl and I were holding hands. He pulled me close and kissed me. His heart monitor began beeping.

"Mr. Nightingale, are you feeling pain?" the nurse asked as she checked the machine.

"No, I just kissed my wife." Earl smiled.

"I don't think that had anything to do with it."

"Sure it did. Let me show you." I leaned down and he kissed me again. The monitor showed irregular activity and the beeping sound began again.

"See," he beamed, "My heart skips a beat every time I kiss that girl."

They all laughed and said that was pretty unusual, but very nice.

By Friday night, Earl was moved from intensive care to a regular room to complete his recovery and begin exercising in preparation for his release.

We anticipated it would be mid-week. Earl vowed he would return home no later than Tuesday. We had dinner together that night and watched TV. Earl was sitting comfortably in a chair, his disposition returned to normal. A man who appreciated good food, he had complained earlier about the food they'd served him. He looked at me and said, "You look like hell."

"Well, thank you very much. It must be all the tender loving care I've gotten this past week."

"When was the last time you slept? Never mind, I know how long it's been. Why don't you go home now and get a good night's rest? You can sleep easy now, I'm just fine. Don't be in a rush to get back here in the morning, either. Just sleep in until you're good and rested.

"But, when you do come, bring those three books on my desk that I'm reading and a couple of yellow legal pads and some pens. Let's get some work done tomorrow. Okay?"

"Okay. Since you're so ambitious, maybe I'll bring some hard boiled eggs and dye and we can color Easter eggs for Sunday."

"Let's skip the eggs. Go home! Sleep!"

I kissed him goodnight and left him sitting there with a big grin on his face, and the TV remote in his hand.

I drove home. I guess I had no idea how exhausted I really was. I no sooner lay down, than I was out like a light. I slept peacefully and awakened refreshed and happy.

I listened to cheerful music as I showered, dressed, gathered up Earl's books and headed back to the hospital.

It was the Saturday before Easter. And, as I pulled out of our driveway, I noticed how beautiful the world looked that morning. Springtime had arrived with all of its splendor. Everywhere I looked, I saw abundant blossoms. The promise of renewal that Easter brings was evident all around me.

I remember feeling so relieved and thankful that surgery was over, that Earl had done so remarkably well and he'd be healthy and back home with me for a long time.

Today was a special day. And we were going to spend it together, watching television and sharing meals; all without nurses and doctors monitoring our every move. I had much to be grateful for.

The hospital parking lot was already full. But I found a spot at the end of the row and under a tree, no less. I gathered up the books and supplies, opened the door of the car, looked down and saw a bright, shiny penny lying on the ground. I didn't even pause to pick it up. Instead, I stepped over it thinking, "I have all the good luck I'll ever need. Let someone else have it."

I remember looking at the clock as I greeted the receptionist. It was about 10:40 a.m. I pushed the elevator button and shifted my books. The elevator door opened and I rode up to Earl's floor.

I noticed that most of the patients had gone home; I supposed, because of the holiday. There weren't any nurses at their station, either.

I waltzed into Earl's room full of cheer and fun, dropped my stuff in the chair and came around the foot of the bed. As I did, I reached over, took hold of Earl's big toe, gave it a wiggle and said, "She's baa-aack."

At first, I thought he was napping. Then a terrible fear gripped my heart as I looked at his face. His eyes were open; but there was something terribly wrong with him.

I grasped his hand and put my other hand on his head. I spoke his name and told him I was there. He squeezed my hand and tried to speak. But all he could do was mumble. I could tell from his eyes that he was in danger.

I had seen him like this three years earlier. At that time, he had been going through severe stress. And one morning, he had a few moments that scared the hell out of both of us. His eyes looked the same way now as they had then.

I had rushed him to the hospital, and the episode had passed quickly. After a thorough examination, we had been told that he'd had a TIA, a transient ischemic attack.

It was described to us as a brief interruption of the blood supply to part of the brain that results in temporary impairment of vision, speech, sensation or movement. We were told that these TIA's can last several minutes or hours. In our case it had lasted only a few minutes and he was fine after that. I was sure it would go away this time, too.

I had Earl's hand and he drew mine up to his face. My heart was pounding loudly in my ears. I kissed him on the forehead and told him not to worry, I'd be right back with help. I ran out into the hall, looking both ways for someone.

I saw a nurse walking down the hall and called out to her. She finally turned around and seemed irritated that I was pursuing her. Couldn't I see that she was "busy"?

"Why isn't someone with my husband?" I demanded, pulling her toward the room. "He's in bad trouble!"

She looked at me as if I were crazy. "There's no need for anyone to be with your husband, Mrs. Nightingale. There's nothing wrong with him. He did say he felt a little strange and sick to his stomach after his breakfast. He thought something was going wrong.

"But I assured him that what he was feeling was not unusual," she rattled on. "After all, he's been through a great deal and he's still on medication and all.

"I did call the doctor for him, as he asked. But he's doing a cath. We've also put in a call for the neurologist. One of them will be here as soon as he's free. But I can assure you, your husband is just fine."

"I'm not trying to tell you how to do your job. But I know my husband and he's in big trouble. He needs help." I was pulling her down the hall.

We got back to the room, just as the neurologist arrived. He began examining Earl. The nurse was trying to assure us that Earl had been fine the last time she checked.

Earl could respond to the doctor's instructions. He could lift his arms and legs, one side better than the other. All the while, he was holding my hand very tightly. I knew he was scared. I was too.

But I tried to reassure Earl, as well as myself, that everything was alright.

The doctor seemed pleased with Earl's responses to his commands. Then he asked Earl how he felt. Earl struggled to speak and finally mumbled something barely intelligible.

The doctor turned to me, "Do you understand what he said?"

"I think he said, `Son of a bitch! I can't talk.'"

"Oh. Well, we'll have to take him to x-ray and find out what's wrong," he said, casually. Neither he nor the nurse seemed to have a sense of urgency or concern.

"Don't worry, Honey," I said. "Everything is going to be okay. Your medication is probably screwed up, or something else very simple. But we'll fix it, and everything will be okay. This is like the time in Naples, and that only lasted a few minutes. You're gonna be fine, I promise. I love you."

Being a Saturday and the day before the holiday, it appeared that the hospital was incredibly short-handed. The nurse asked me to help wheel Earl's bed down to x-ray. I was grateful to be able to do something – anything. I was terrified by now and kept praying that everything would be okay.

I sat outside the x-ray room and waited. Time stood still. Down the hall, the doors swung open, as Earl's cardiologist rushed to my side. He looked concerned. He liked Earl and he didn't like what was happening.

"Must have thrown a clot," he said. "But if so, we'll find out where it is and, if it's in the right place, we'll get rid of it and he'll be all right. If it isn't, well, he could remain in this state and yet get physically well. Or – he could die."

Well, of course, he could die – we all could die. But, of course, he won't, I told myself. I struggled for my sanity and my defenses rose with a bad joke.

"I don't believe Earl can die," I said nervously. "I personally believe he's an alien. You'll see. He heals fast and is a good fighter.

"We've been in lots of tight jams and we're good fighters and we always win. I know you're doing your best, and I know he'll be fine."

Just as the nurse wheeled Earl out of x-ray, my older daughter, Kim, arrived. I was grateful to see her and have her there with me. No one else seemed to be around, so Kim and I helped the nurse push Earl's bed to the elevator.

"Have you medicated him?" I asked. "He seems to be in such a deep sleep."

"No, it's just typical of a stroke," she said.

Stroke. There it was. That was the first time, I suppose, I really considered that reality. My mind had jumped passed that possibility when I found him, choosing instead to believe it was another TIA that would go away. And certainly, no one else had given any indication that's what had happened.

I needed Earl to talk to now. I was frightened beyond any fear I had ever known. I didn't know what to do. He was my life.

We reached Earl's room. By now, a couple of nurses had come to the floor from somewhere to help move him back onto his bed. Kim and I stepped out into the hall to give them more room.

Suddenly there was a loud shout, "Code!" The word hung loudly in the air for a moment, then turned and hit me in the chest and the pit of my stomach. I couldn't move or breathe. Kim grabbed my arm.

Just minutes earlier, the hospital had seemed deserted. Now, people were coming from everywhere; people running with a look of serious resolve. It seemed like hundreds of people, all running, running, running.

I felt like three or four people wrapped up into one. One of me was stricken with the most intense fear and pain I have ever felt. My entire body felt as though it was being torn apart by some internal explosion. My heart was pounding and my head throbbing. I thought for the first time, "He's going to die!"

Another me was busy taking mental notes; observing the faces and intentions of the nurses and doctors. I remember saying to Kim, "Isn't it amazing to see all those people with just one single purpose: trying to save Earl's life." That part of me was proud of them.

The third me was trying to get out and run far away from what was happening; while at the same time, a fourth was trying desperately to keep myself all together and deal with and understand what was going on. The pain ... the pain was so intense.

Someone came out of the room just then; took me by the arm, and led me down the hall away from the room and Earl. They were taking in the defibrillator.

I went over to the window. I clutched the window frame for support. I was shaking all over and crying.

I began to pray, not just words into the Great Unknown as I had all of my life, but for the first time, I spoke directly to God. Not only did I know He could hear me, I could actually feel His presence. He was so close. It was so easy to talk to Him.

I told Him I didn't want Earl to suffer. I didn't want him to be locked into a body that wouldn't function or speak. Earl had dreaded that might happen to him one day and vowed that if it ever did and there was a way to end it, he would.

I asked God to give Earl back to me whole and healthy, if it was His will. But if not, to please take him quickly, so that he wouldn't suffer.

At once, I was comforted by a warm feeling of peace. I knew that God had answered my prayer. I just didn't know what the answer was.

The doctor came down the hall just then and said, "We got him back. It took ten times but we got him back."

I sighed a big sigh of relief, blew my nose, wiped my eyes and said, "Thank you. May I see him now?"

The doctor put his arm around my shoulder and guided me back to the elevator. "He's on his way back to ICCU," he said. "I'll take you there so you can be with him."

Back in ICCU, I felt confident everything was under control and Earl would live. I went in and gave him a hug and a kiss. "I love you. Please don't be afraid."

I turned to the neurologist and asked what the x-ray had showed. He led me out into the hall, "Nothing. We saw nothing."

Earl's cardiologist put his hand on my arm and told me in a very soft and serious voice, they didn't have much more than "life".

He said that if they didn't have better than that in six hours or so, we'd have some serious decisions to make. He asked if I was strong enough to make that kind of decision.

Before I could answer, the nurse called out that she was losing him.

I rushed inside, grabbed Earl's hand and pressed it to my chest. I wanted to hang on, to hold him back, to give him my life if that's what it took. I'd do anything to keep him with me. I touched my lips to his forehead, my tears falling on his face.

I told him how much I loved him now and how much I'd love him forever. He squeezed my hand, nodded his head. And then – he was gone.

I sat next to the bed with my head on Earl's chest, still holding his hand. I never wanted to leave or even move into the next moment in time. Nothing seemed real. I didn't know what to do, and Earl was getting so cold.

I pulled the covers up around him. His blue eyes were still open. I closed them, kissed him one more time and left the room.

The doctor told me I had to sign some papers at the desk. I noticed that the nurses and doctors were crying. They took turns hugging me and telling me how sorry they all were and what a fine man Earl had been. Earl hadn't been just another patient who didn't make it.

By two o'clock in the afternoon I was back home, staring at the phone and dreading the thought of calling Earl's children to tell them their father was dead.

It all still seemed unreal. I didn't believe it and I'd been there. Maybe there was a mistake and he wasn't really dead. Maybe I should wait. But it was real and I made the calls.

Shortly after I talked to them, the phone began ringing. Someone at the hospital called, then the mortuary, then someone who had heard that Earl had died and wanted to know if it was true. Then the newspaper called and wanted to know if it was true, insisting that I do a press release.

I turned to Kim in cold, utter disbelief. "Do they honestly think we keep press releases in the drawer for any occasion that happens?" Sarcastically I said, "Look under 'D' in the files and see what we have."

Now I was crying angrily. Even now, there was no privacy. I went to our bedroom. Kim went downstairs to the office and in an incredibly short time, returned with a beautiful, freshly written press release. "Where did this come from?" I asked in disbelief.

"I just wrote what Earl would have told me to write."

Earl. Of course. He was our whole world and we were already experiencing the miracle of love. He was still with us. Kim called the paper and local radio station. I called Paul Harvey's office and asked if he would release the news of Earl's death to the world. He agreed.

I went down to the studio and sat at the recording table, as if there I could find the answer to what I should do next. I felt numb and paralyzed.

Lying on the recording table was a cassette that I had dubbed only a month earlier. We had recorded for several hours one Saturday and Earl suggested that I lift one of the messages for "future use".

"Never know when this one might come in handy for someone," he'd said.

I put it in the machine and turned it on, shut my eyes and listened. I could hear the sound of the tape moving through the machine. Then, the studio was filled with the sound of his voice.

Hello, this is Earl Nightingale. . . .One of the most obvious examples of immaturity we see about us is the person who, following a setback or tragedy of some kind, says, "What have I done? Why am I being punished?"

"It's always I – 'What have I done? Why am I being punished?'

"This form of childish selfishness is a form of self-pity that often remains even after a person is supposed to have grown up. It's a lack of maturity, a lack of understanding.

"Nobody is singled out and punished by some cruel fate or vindictive God for his past mistakes. When we make mistakes, sure we have to face the natural consequences of those mistakes, but it is we who made them.

"Perhaps the fault might lie with parents who didn't know how to properly raise a child, or with a broken home. But that's the way the ball happened to bounce. Blaming will do no good whatever.

"And if we're visited by a tragedy through no fault of our own, that's the whole story; we've been visited by a tragedy. Nobody wanted it to happen; everyone's sorry it did happen; but it did happen.

"For a while, it's going to numb us and knock us flat. And the whole world is going to seem like the vestibule to Erebus. But even in the depths of sorrow, we need to look at what happened in its true light. It happened. It had nothing whatever to do with some past sin, nor is it arcane retribution.

"If we feel that we could have – should have – been kinder, less critical, more thoughtful than we were, then let's do something positive about it by being kinder, less critical and more thoughtful from here on out. If we have not been staggered by a tragic personal loss, just knowing that it could occur at any time should make us think a bit about the way we're treating those it has been given us to love.

"When the great hammer blow of tragedy strikes, to ask, 'Why have I been singled out to be punished in this way?' is a kind of Gargantuan conceit.

"The Kennedy family, with two fine sons lost by unprecedented, senseless assassination, a third killed in World War II and the fourth injured in an airplane crash, might well have thought that all the mysterious forces of the universe had gotten together and repeatedly conspired to punish this one family. Instead, their reactions to their repeated tragedies were models and lessons to the world in dignity and maturity.

"The secret in getting over tragedy in a healthy way seems to be in getting rid of the focus on I and doing something for others. This is much easier said than done. But difficult as it may be, it seems to be the best and quickest cure.

"The sense of loss, the ache, will perhaps never disappear entirely. Like an old wound, it will leave its scar. But scars can be worn with dignity.

"Byron wrote: 'Sorrow preys upon its solitude, and nothing more diverts it from its sad visions of the other world, than calling it at moments back to this. The busy have no time for tears.'"

There it was. My first instruction on how to get through this first day of shock and disbelief.

The next morning, I sat and listened to Paul Harvey as he said:

"Partly personal . . .

"In the fledgling years of radio, all of the pictures you saw in your living room were painted with words. And there were memorable, mellifluent voices that brought those pictures to life: Phil Stewart, Franklin McCormack, and Earl Nightingale.

"In more recent years, Earl has devoted his majestic voice to motivation programs and speeches. The sonorous song of the Nightingale ... is still this morning. Earl died following heart surgery in Scottsdale, Arizona.

"But through a library of recordings, his worthy admonitions will echo endlessly, prodding us all to do more than we can and to be more than we are."

Now, that I'd seen it on TV, read it in the newspaper and heard Paul Harvey say it on the radio, it must be true. Earl must really be dead. Why was this so hard to believe?

Chapter 13

*A fire celestial, chaste, refin'd,
Conceiv'd and kindled in the mind,
Which, having found an equal flame,
Unites, and both become the same.*
Jonathan Swift (1713)

A few weeks passed. Earl was gone. And the days and nights without him were excruciatingly painful. I found myself playing that same type of selfish mental game he'd warned against in that last recording. I blamed myself for his death. If I had lied to him about not having any balloons left, that he had just scratched the surface of all the things I wanted, he would have stayed longer.

One night, I was watching a TV program about firemen. It was a very emotional story about one particular fireman who had been badly burned in a fire. He died after suffering through several operations.

As if the tragedy of this man's death weren't enough, the story was told by his wife. I don't know what period of time had passed since his death. But she told the story with bravery and dignity, holding back the pain, grief and suffering she was experiencing. I wept for her, for him, for Earl, for myself.

No one can know – unless you've been there – what it's like to watch the person who holds your life in his hands, suffer and die. The passage of time doesn't matter. It will always hurt. It will always be difficult to talk about or remember, without choking back the tears.

As the television story unfolded, the fireman was remembered and laid to rest. It was a beautiful tribute to this man who had risked his life every day for people he did not know. I thought to myself, he probably did it because he was just a great guy.

There was a great funeral procession with bagpipes and mourners lining the street. And there was a beautiful church service. And all of the people whose lives he had touched in someway lighted candles and surrounded his wife and family, remembering him with love and appreciation.

That's when I wept just for Earl and myself.

I believe it's wrong for us to compare anyone with another person. Each of us is a unique and special individual who brings to life's experiences whatever he or she has been given to bring. Whatever the contribution, great or small, noticed or unnoticed, it's important. Each of us is a distinctive part of the great canvas covering time and the Universe. We're really too involved and too close to see the big picture. But it's there, with each of us playing an important role.

I didn't compare the fireman with my husband. But each, in his own way, responded to the emergencies in other people's lives — sometimes with something routine; other times, with something life-saving.

Earl was only a child when his interest in people and life set him on his inquisitive journey. It took him around the world, to touch millions of people's lives. Yet at age 68, after a lifetime of service, I laid him to rest, supported only by my children and three friends.

Earl didn't care for the traditional ceremonial treatment of death. He didn't want anyone to see him, didn't want a funeral and wanted to be cremated.

But surely, out of all the millions of lives he touched – and in some instances, changed dramatically for the better – someone could have offered to be there. I received phone calls and a few flowers, along with a ton of sympathy cards and letters of condolence from strangers. But it was lonely and painful as I walked through our home.

I cried and sometimes screamed, hoping that I'd get the attention of God and that He, in His divine love and compassion, would strike me dead and the pain would stop.

A few weeks after Earl died, his late partner's son came to visit. He was now at the helm of the company Earl and his father had built. It was only natural that he would extend his sympathy and concern for me in person.

I was glad to see him. I asked if he would help me organize a tribute to Earl, perhaps in Chicago, where the company was headquartered, and where Earl had spent so many of his years in radio.

I'll never forget his cold, detached response. He had no desire to organize any kind of memorial in Earl's honor, he said. Earl had been dead now a couple of weeks. There wasn't a body. Why in the world would he organize a tribute?

Stunned and pained, I asked why he had made the trip. His answer was simple. He said he wanted to see if Earl had created any work the company didn't know about, work they could market now that he was dead.

If astronomers were searching for black holes, they could have found one in the pit of my stomach. I felt as if I were falling and no one was there to save me. I wanted to lash out, screaming that if it weren't for Earl, this man probably wouldn't be running a company at all; not to mention a multi-million dollar enterprise.

By contrast, Earl had been a successful radio commentator, the voice of *Sky King* and the host of his own TV show. He had owned an insurance company and had written *The Strangest Secret.* Later, he co-founded the corporation to fill the orders for the book.

For the first 10 or 15 years, Earl Nightingale programs generated the company's only revenue and paid everyone's salaries. His work fed not only the Nightingale family, but his partner's as well.

In 25 years, the company had grown to an estimated 36-million dollar enterprise, which this man inherited through his father's death. And he saw no reason for a tribute.

He just wanted to know if there was more money to be made from Earl Nightingale.

More than ever, after that incident, I felt an overwhelming need to publicly acknowledge that Earl had existed and had made a difference in the world.

Weeks later, I arranged for a tribute to be presented in Dallas at a gathering of the National Speakers Association (NSA). I was assisted by the outgoing president, Jim Cathcart; a man I had never met. Many fellow speakers attended.

Cathcart told about Earl's influence on his life. He was followed by a videotaped message from *Psychology of Winning* author, Dr. Denis Waitley – the first person other than Earl to produce motivational programs for Nightingale-Conant.

I addressed the audience, trying to relate the kind of man Earl was to me and presented a video of photos from our album, showing the personal side of Earl. I closed with a poem by Father Michael Lennon:

> *When I come to the end of the road*
> *and the sun has set for me*
> *I want no rites in a gloom-filled room;*
> *Why cry for a soul set free?*
>
> *Miss me a little, but not too long*
> *and not with your head bowed low;*
> *Remember the love that we once shared;*
> *Miss me – but let me go.*
>
> *For this is a journey we all must take;*
> *And each must go alone.*
> *It's all a part of the Master's plan,*
> *a step on the road to home.*
>
> *When you're lonely and sick of heart,*
> *go to the friends we know;*
> *And bury your sorrows in doing good deeds.*
> *Miss me – but let me go.*

For the next 45 minutes, I received warm hugs and heard treasured stories of how Earl had touched the lives of these strangers. They expressed their grief and loss; and warmly allowed me to express mine. The much-loved Earl had finally been honored; and beautifully so.

The next morning, my daughters and I boarded our flight back to Phoenix – lonely Phoenix, where no one called or visited any more.

The suddenness of Earl's death and the lack of any real ceremony had left me in a state of confusion. There had been no closure. I would wake up in the night and think that I had figured out what had gone wrong. I'd get out of bed and pour over the medical reports from the hospital. I had moments when I really believed that if I could figure out what went wrong, it could be fixed and Earl would be alive again. I really believed that.

One night during a storm, an electrical surge caused the CD player in Earl's office to start playing. It came on loudly. I awoke with a start, and thought his death had been a bad dream. I raced down the hall, believing when I got to his office I'd find him there at the typewriter, just like all the other nights when he couldn't sleep.

At times, I'd remember the penny I didn't pick up at the hospital that morning — and wonder if I should have.
One night, I had gone to our room to undress for bed. Suddenly, I had an incredible pain in my head and severe nausea. I rushed to the toilet and knelt there, retching. I thought, "My God, this is what Earl felt before he died." I felt as though in our unity, our oneness, that all the pain had left his body when he died and had at last manifested itself in me. It was a rough night.

In the morning, my head had stopped hurting. But my entire body ached. The pain I'd felt when Earl was dying was now intensifying. My skin hurt so badly, I couldn't bear to be touched. I told my brother, John, I finally knew what it meant to have a broken heart. I never knew how I'd feel from day to day. I'd bounce back and forth between feelings of intense pain, despair and complete devastation.

Then unexpectedly, I would experience moments of great joy for Earl. He had been released from a sick body and had gone on to the great "mystery," as he put it so often.

As for me, it seemed that when Earl died, all the lights went out in the world. I looked around for something of value to make my prolonged stay on Planet Earth worthwhile without him.

As I inventoried my life, I realized that sharing it with Earl had made it all worthwhile. All the big and little acquisitions were only important when he was here, because we had desired and planned for them together. Now that he was gone, there was little value in what was left behind.

Dealing with lawyers, you're brought face to face with your own mortality. It's then, you realize, these "things" we work so hard to acquire must ultimately be left behind. How blindingly clear it becomes that we take nothing of worldly value into our next experience. And we leave nothing behind; nothing, except love.

I received a ton of mail from well-meaning strangers, who sent cards and booklets about death. Bless them, they wanted to ease my pain. But they could only guess what I was feeling.

Some of their hopeful messages would cheerfully tell me I'd get over it; it just took time. Some even had schedules, predicting what I would feel at different weeks or months. It was as though grief were a charted, predictable journey. All you had to do was look at where you were, measure your degree of pain; and you would be able to know what would happen next – or how you would feel at the next point in time. Someone had even come up with a handy-dandy guide to get you through the death experience — and back to "normal."

After a few weeks, I felt I had done everything that was expected of me: paperwork, phone calls and proper attitude.

It was Friday and now I wanted to die. I wanted to be with Earl. I wanted and needed to escape my pain. And death was as far away as I could imagine.

I believed death was the only place there was no pain; that God or Earl would come for me, if only I willed it and allowed it to happen.

By evening, I had a raging fever and couldn't keep anything in my stomach. It was a rugged weekend. But, when Monday morning came, I was still alive.

A small voice, deep inside of me, let me know I hadn't been invited to the other side. It wasn't time. And I knew both God and Earl would have been terribly upset if I failed to live out the rest of my life. I could see them looking at each other and shaking their heads saying, "I really thought she could do the job."

So, I wasn't supposed to die yet. I accepted that. But I couldn't deal with what I was feeling. I was sure I was losing my mind and wouldn't be able to make it through another day.

I called Earl's cardiologist and asked him to refer me to a psychiatrist. He told me he was sure I didn't need one; but suggested that I join a grief support group that met near my home. They were meeting that night.

There probably were 20 people there. We sat in a circle and the moderator began by telling us why she was qualified to speak on the subject. Her husband had been lost in the war and she'd had to deal with the unknown for seven years. Then, we each took turns telling about our loss.

One man had been coming to the group for *eight years*. I wondered why he hadn't moved on to phase two, three and four like the people who prescribed the grieving process had said I would.

An elderly man sat next to me. He leaned over and told me that he was going on a cruise that next week. "That's nice." I smiled.

"But, I feel guilty about going."

"Then don't go."

"Well, I really want to go. But you know, well, my wife died. And here I am thinking about a cruise."

"I think you should go."

"I don't know."

"Look," I said, "It's been longer for you than it has for me. And that guy over there has had eight years to think about it. One thing seems to be clear; and you need to think about it: You can stay home from the cruise, and that guy can come here every week for the rest of his life, and we can all dress in black or red, laugh or cry. It doesn't matter. Our spouses aren't coming back."

The man sat back in his chair – silent.

After everyone "shared", we adjourned for coffee and donuts. I approached the moderator and asked if we had run out of time.

"No, everyone shared. Did you want to say something else?"

"No, I didn't want to say anything else. But where's the hope?"

"What hope?" she seemed bewildered.

"The hope – the encouragement that this is part of life and that we can find a way to deal with our loss."

"We come here to share our grief," she said. "Come back next week, you'll feel better."

"Like the man who's made it his life for eight years? No thank you."

The only thing that worked for me was to pray for peace, strength, courage and insight. And it came, one day at a time. I knew to survive this, I would have to have God's help. I wouldn't last a minute without it.

As the weeks went by, Earl's shoes and socks still lay on the floor by his desk. His khaki pants were still over the back of the chair where he'd placed them the night before he went to the hospital. His M&Ms were there on the desk and his books were scattered, awaiting his return. I looked in the freezer, and there were the two ice cream containers left over from his birthday. There were dents in the side of the containers where his big hand had squeezed the sides while he ate from the carton with the spoon. His toothpaste lay flattened out on the sink in the bathroom.

Things looked pretty much the same as before he left. But instead of bringing him home, I brought a container with his ashes. And now, it sat on the high shelf of his study.

I missed Earl, the man. I missed the laughter and tears; the good times and the bickering, the dinners and lunches and midnight snacks. I missed going out on the terrace with him at night and sitting on our big chaise looking out into the night sky and wondering about the universe and eternity. I was jealous that he "knew" and I didn't.

Chapter 14

Dost thou not perceive that all creatures both in Heaven and earth prize God, and the birds also, extending their wings?
The Koran, xxiv

Through the years – somewhere between my Catholic experience and the countless other religious explorations – I had found the answer to the question I wondered about as a child: Which theology best suited me?

Like Earl, who'd found the answer to his question regarding success in all the great writings of the world, I found that I kept hearing my answer over and over again at each church I attended. No matter the denomination, sooner or later the minister or priest quoted John 14:6 – "Jesus said to him, 'I am the way, the truth, and the life. No one comes to the Father except through Me.'"

Once I made that discovery and it rang true to my heart, my spiritual growth expanded rapidly. Having a direct line to God through Jesus and cutting out all the middle men on Earth was great!

Now, since Earl's death, my prayers not only brought me tremendous peace but a presence of the Lord to hold me up and guide me through the darkness. In addition to prayer, I listened to Earl's voice on our many tapes. They gave me great comfort. On the surface, I had a positive mental attitude. And I was able to fool the world into thinking I was coping just fine. But inside, I was still a basket case! I felt like I still hosted those multiple personalities who revealed themselves to me at the hospital.

Noya and Terry called. They had moved to Holland from South Africa and were terribly concerned for me and how I was handling my loss. Noya said she'd come to be with me.

They called back later and said they felt it would be better for me if I came and stayed with them a while. I promised as soon as I took care of things at home that needed immediate attention, I would come. But, I really had no desire to go.

As time passed, I kept busy filling everyone's needs but my own. My days were jam-packed. But when five o'clock came, I was alone, missing Earl. I kept expecting to see him in his favorite chair, cup of coffee in hand, watching the five o'clock news.

So, I filled up the evenings, working and watching the clock until it was late enough and I was tired enough to fall asleep. Sometimes I had no dreams or I'd dream that Earl was there visiting me, walking me through the recovery process. I would awaken in the morning, wishing I could just sleep through this whole thing until the pain ended.

Weekends were absolutely the worst. I hated Fridays most of all. But then, Saturdays were always a marker, a reminder of Earl's death. After weeks of suffering, I decided to find a way to deal with the pain of the weekend. I didn't drink, except on social occasions because I never wanted to be out of control. I had just as strong of a dislike for taking drugs, even when sick. I was left with only one other escape. I ran away.

Fortunately, I had acquired lots of frequent flyer miles. I made plans to go somewhere every Friday. I visited my friend Linda in Oregon, other friends in California and Florida. I returned home to Ohio to visit my mother. I kept one step ahead of my pain.

My escapes were almost as bad as alcohol or drugs. I found that I had to run faster and faster, farther and farther; because no matter where I ran, the pain was still there.

One day I received a card from a friend of ours, Dennis Hay, in Alaska. He had been a big fan of Earl's. We had visited Dennis' fishing camp in Elfin Cove in 1985 and had enjoyed the peace of the place as well as the great salmon and halibut catches.

The folks at Elfin Cove extended their condolences and Dennis wondered if perhaps I would like to "get away to a quiet place". Arte Wolfe, the wildlife photographer, and other fun guests would be there in June.

Until then, my escapes had been to safe havens, like visits to close friends and family. I was so badly shaken, every trip I made took enormous courage. But I was keenly aware that I would have to rejoin the world and begin venturing out with others. I accepted Dennis' invitation.

Not ready to go solo, I took along my 13-year-old grandson, Dan. We flew to Seattle and changed planes to Juneau, where we were picked up by seaplane and flown to Elfin Cove.

The trip brought back a rush of memories. I found it difficult to visit a place where Earl and I had been and where we had enjoyed ourselves so much.

I recalled the rainy day Dennis took a picture of Earl and me in our rain gear, sitting on a log. We loved the memory so much, we had Christmas cards made from the picture to send to all of our friends. I fought hard to keep Danny from knowing how painful it was for me to be there without Earl.

Every day, we were up early and out in our boats to fish or take pictures. At first, the weather was rainy and cold. And each day was difficult for me; even though I was surrounded by old and new friends.

About halfway through the week, I found my emotions very hard to contain. Earlier in the day, I had fought back tears on several occasions. By the time dinner was over, all I could think of was how much I needed a hug. Earl had been generous with his hugs and I would have given anything for one that day.

After dinner, the guests retired to the great, cozy room downstairs where there was a fire in the wood stove. A couple of the guests sat playing cards while the rest of us set up for videos. The first movie began and I could feel the tears choking my throat. I could hardly breathe. I felt like the room was closing in and I wanted to scream.

I got up, put on my coat and gloves and left the lodge. It wouldn't get dark until well after midnight; so I knew I had plenty of time.

A boardwalk runs the rim of the cove and I took off, walking at top speed. The cold air against my face was a welcome relief. I completely circled the village in no time and started on trip number two. After a second round, I still felt wired and decided to take the boardwalk that led off into the interior of the island.

I had gone some distance when I heard what sounded like large, unfriendly dogs barking. I was unhappy, yes, but not reckless. Life was tough enough. I wasn't about to have an encounter with some large, vicious animal. I almost smiled when I realized how my sense of survival was still intact and had, for a moment, rescued me from my misery. I turned around and headed back.

I returned to the boardwalk area above the cove where the boats were docked. There was a young woman squatting down, filling a tea kettle with a hose. She was in jeans, but well-groomed.

She smiled at me. "Hi, where are you staying?"

I smiled back. "Boy, this place sure is small. Guess strangers really stick out, huh?"

"Yes, you do," she replied.

"I'm down at the Elfin Cove Fishing Lodge, at Dennis Hay's place."

"Want a drink?" she asked.

"I'll take tea if you have it," I said, surprising myself.

"Sure. Come on in. It's moving day for me. You're my first guest. My name is Sally."

We went into a small one-room building. There was a table, a stove, a bed, a couple of dressers and chairs. A clarinet lay on the table.

"Who plays?" I asked.

"I do," she smiled.

She fixed tea for me and popped open a can of beer for herself. We went back outside and sat on a deck, propped up our feet on the rail and looked down at the boats docked below. It was about 9:30 in the evening, but still light.

I asked her what she was doing there and where she'd come from. She told me she was divorced and was going about her routine as a travel agent in Sitka, when she just decided one day to quit and "go fishing."

"So, that's what I do," she said.

"What?" I said, stupidly.

"I go fishing. I'm a commercial fisherwoman."

I looked in amazement at her. She looked so ordinary – like a city girl. "You fish?!" I asked, dumbfounded.

"Yes, I fish. I love it. My boyfriend and I lived aboard a boat down there for a year. But it's rough and cold. So when this place became available, we grabbed it. He's in getting supplies. We just moved in today."

She went on for a while about herself and her boyfriend. And then she asked why I was there. Since I didn't know her and she wasn't going to be a part of my life, I felt safe telling her my story. She looked like she really knew what I was experiencing, excused herself and went inside.

Moments later, she returned with a letter from her sister, who'd recently lost her husband. Her sister was in her 30s. She described in depth what she was going through emotionally. Her words were my words. The tears came. Sally didn't mind.

After she read the letter, Sally said she felt the letter was as much for me as it was for her. I thanked her for sharing it with me. I felt less alone.

I finished my tea and said I had to leave before Dan worried that his grandma had been eaten by bears or something. We chuckled. Thanking her for her hospitality, I walked to the end of the deck and turned to leave.

"Before you go," she said, "I have something for you." She walked over, put her arms around me and gave me a world-class hug. "You're gonna be all right," she promised.

"Thank you. Thank you for everything," I said, grateful that God had sent me the hug I needed so badly. I headed back to the lodge.

The night air was cold. The trees and ferns were so green and lush; a perfect place to pause and say a prayer of thanksgiving.

"I got the message, Lord," I prayed. "No matter where I am, you know what I always need – even if it's just a hug and I'm on a tiny island in Alaska. Thank you for Sally and thanks for the hug."

The guests were watching movies when I arrived at the lodge, laughing and enjoying the evening. I said good night to everyone and returned to our room.

Dan had been worn out from our day on the boats and his 50-pound catch. He had crashed earlier. I listened to his peaceful breathing from his bed across the room. I pulled the comforter up over my shoulders and drifted off to sleep. I slept well that night, secure once again in the knowledge that I am not alone. God is with me always.

The weeks passed. I kept in close contact with God. But on an earthly plane, nothing changed for me. I wasn't on schedule with my recovery, as far as the world was concerned. I had responded to the many demands that were placed on me, and I had met my business and estate responsibilities. But emotionally, I had only been able to accomplish one thing, with all my racing about: accepting Earl's death.

I finally realized that Earl was not coming back. But, I didn't know what to do about it. How was I going to live out the rest of my life? What happened to my "holiday on earth"? How could I find my "journey into meaning" without Earl? I had trouble making it through the endless days and nights.

Earl had become my life, my thoughts, my dreams, my future. And now, I didn't have a clue where I was or where I was suppose to go. I felt abandoned on the path and I didn't know if I could continue the trip alone.

I desperately needed some physical evidence that I was strong enough to make it on my own. I needed to prove to myself that I was strong enough to go on alone.

Noya, dear friend that she is, continued to call. "Deanna, when will you come?" she persisted.

This time I said, "I'm ready, Noya. I have my tickets."

And so, after six months, I set out to see some of Europe. I had never been to Europe and I speak only English. I saw this trip as my physical evidence that I could journey out into a foreign world where people speak a language different from mine, be on my own and survive without Earl. I believed that accomplishing this would give me the proof I needed.

My brother, John, said I was brave to go to a foreign land where people spoke a different language.

I called it my trip to Des Moines. I'd never been there, either. "It's really all the same," I explained. "I'll go to the airport, get on a plane, and it will take off.

"Later, it will land and I'll be someplace I've never been before, like Des Moines. And because I have been speaking a language different from most people most of my life, it shouldn't be a big deal."

I decided to take the Concorde, because it would get me there quickly. I wasn't into savoring life's experiences just then. I just wanted to get there and get on with it. If I could just go fast enough and far enough, I could leave all the pain behind. I flew from Phoenix to Denver and spent the night. Early the next morning, I boarded a plane for Washington, D.C.

I sat on the left side of the plane, along side an attractive woman in a United Airlines uniform. Her name was Jo Beth. As we ate breakfast, we chatted about our lives. She told me she was a wife and mother who one day decided to follow her life's dream and pursue an aeronautical career. Now she was a captain, flying commercial planes. Her story was interesting and I enjoyed speaking with her.

She asked about my life.

I told her what circumstances had led me to this flight. She too, thought it was brave of me to go to Europe alone so soon after Earl's death. I laughingly told her about it being my "trip to Des Moines."

Breakfast over, we sat sipping tea. The loudspeaker came on and the captain welcomed us to the flight. He gave us all the stats: temperatures, air speed, tail winds, approximate time of arrival. Then he said, "And for those of you seated on the left side of the plane, take a look out of your window." I instinctively looked. "You will see that we are presently flying over Des Moines," he announced.

Jo Beth and I stared at each other and then burst out laughing.

"I make this trip all the time," she said. "I've never heard anyone announce Des Moines before," she said.

"Nor have I," I said.

Then she said, with a serious note, "This is some trip you're taking, my dear. And that announcement was just for you."

My journey alone continued.

Chapter 15

*I have been a wanderer among distant fields,
I have sailed down mighty rivers.*
P.B. Shelley (1818)

A flight on the Concorde had been on our list of "things to do". So, it seemed appropriate to begin my special journey on this special aircraft. The supersonic flight from Washington to London can only be described as a "real blast!!"

Even though I'd told my kids the flight would be exciting, I couldn't possibly have anticipated the thrill of the actual experience. I'd flown in planes of all sizes and shapes – from Australian helicopters to Alaskan seaplanes. Nothing compared with the Concorde.

The plane was lovelier and larger than I expected. Friends had told me it would be small and cramped. It was smaller, to be sure; but quite lovely with gray leather upholstery and indirect lighting. The attendants were very British and very polite. I looked outside the tiny windows and prepared myself for a sensational journey.

On previous flights overseas, I had waited two hours or more to take off from JFK. Here at Dulles in Washington, however, we quickly taxied into position at the end of the runway, paused momentarily and fired the jets. Forty-five seconds later, we were on our way. The ground dropped quickly beneath us. Soon we could see only waterways, then clouds, blue sky, another layer of clouds and then just blueness and the curvature of the earth.

On the bulkhead wall, our mileage, mach speed and altitude clicked off. This was no ordinary plane ride. We didn't level off; we just kept going up. The man sitting next to me said, as we hit Mach 2, "That's it. We're on the edge of space."

I felt sick to my stomach and ready to cry. I realized I was afraid without Earl at my side. Once again, I was completely out of control. I visualized what it would be like not to come back. Suddenly, June Lockhart, Dr. Smith and boy genius Will Robinson were all out there with us – *Lost in Space*.

Now might be a perfect time to change drinks, I thought. The champagne was terrific; but it seemed a little light. This called for something more powerful.

We reached 58,000 feet and were going 1,360 miles an hour when I decided to let go and enjoy the experience, especially since my options were minimal.

About three and a half hours later, we touched down at Heathrow Airport in London like "a butterfly with sore feet." It was great. I couldn't wait to do it again on my return home.

So far, I'd survived the trip.

I checked into the airport Sheraton and immediately was reminded that I was traveling alone. I'd worn boots that day and now my feet were so badly swollen I couldn't get them out of my boots.

Earl always said we were problem solvers. Here was one I sure needed his help with. After exhausting all possibilities, I called the bellman and explained my plight. He arrived, removed my boots and left with a smile, saying his wife had the same problem when she flew. He hoped she realized how lucky she was to still have him around. I agreed and thanked him.

I got up early the next day for the next leg of my trip – London to Amsterdam. I waited for the airport bus, along with another young man. Each time a bus arrived, we both got on – only to discover it was the wrong bus. After several mistaken attempts, he asked if I was flying to New York.

I said, "No. What makes you think I'm going to New York?"

"Because I can tell you're an American," he smiled. He'd just come from Moscow. He'd also been to Poland and Hungary. As he characterized it, he "got around a lot".

He had to get to New York as soon as possible. He was taking the Concorde.

"I want to ask you what you do," I said. "But if you're a spy or something, I'd rather not know." I wasn't ready for that intense of an adventure.

He laughed and produced a business card. He was an international financial planner for Citibank. We chatted all the way to the airport and then headed off in different directions.

A short time later, I boarded my KLM flight to Amsterdam. The plane was nice. But I noticed a difference in the attitude of the attendants. They seemed abrupt and not as friendly. Luckily, it was a short flight.

I waited forever for my luggage. But once I passed through customs, I was greeted at last by my old friends, Terry and Noya. After a quick car ride, we arrived at their home – a three story condo.

My room was on the third level; spacious and wonderful feeling. As the room belonged to their girls, it felt like being with family. My room had a window that overlooked the drive and parking area. I spent long periods of time staring out this window at the children playing loudly. They all had white-blonde hair; all carried long pea-shooter type weapons and rode bikes with a vengeance.

In the weeks ahead, I began to see them as aggressive, little army men. They were always marching, destroying, screaming. It was the first and only time in my life, I didn't like being around children.

I found the adults to be equally aggressive on the road in their cars. It was a terrifying experience. When on their bikes, they thought nothing of bumping into you or running you off the sidewalks. The merchants neither smiled nor greeted their customers and I became tense as the days went by. Noya constantly cautioned me against leaving things in the car or at home.

I tried all my American tricks, like smiling at everyone I met. But it didn't work. I was the enemy, a smiling fool.

I couldn't sleep at night. I began each day, marking time on my calendar. I counted the days left and counted them again – just in case I had miscalculated the night before.

I practiced what Erich Fromm called the "last freedom," the frontier of the mind. I pretended I was somewhere else – past or future. I stopped smiling and my soul was immobilized. Terry said I looked like my lights were going out.

I called my friends, Leana and Friedy, who lived in Hanover, Germany. Leana was a friend of my son, Dayne. I'd known her for many years. She and her husband, Friedy had stayed with Earl and me for several weeks after we moved to Arizona. I wanted them know I was in Holland, and see if they would like to have company.

I also wanted to see their new baby, Kristina. They referred to me as Kristina's American grandma (hers were both dead). They were delighted to hear from me and asked me to come and visit.

I made arrangements to take a train from Sassenheim the following week. Noya said the same train that went to Hanover went on to Berlin, and suggested that we both go to Berlin first. I could get off in Hanover on the way back. She would return to Holland.

Earl had talked so much about how great the train systems are in Europe. Although he never had any first-hand experience, he'd say, "You take a bus and get off. Get on one train, get off. Get on another and so on – There wasn't anywhere one couldn't go. And, it's always best if you can go first class."

Bearing in mind his enthusiasm for trains and thinking how much he'd love the idea if he were alive, we booked reservations. The agent was a very nasty, arrogant man. We wanted a first-class sleeping compartment, since we would travel all night. He checked and all were booked.

He said, "Take first-class cushettes."

"Would it be private?"

"Yes."

"Is there a dining car?"
"Yes."
"Fine."

We bought our tickets and returned home to plan our packing. We would have to carry whatever we took; so our bags would have to be maneuverable.

Our trip began in the evening. We left home, each lugging our one, but extremely heavy, bag. We had tried not to take too much. But even the bare necessities seemed to be heavier than we expected.

We caught a bus in Sassenheim to Lieden, found a locker at the terminal, stuffed our bags in and walked into town to eat. Noya suggested that we just get coffee. We could eat on the train.

I thought we should start out with a full tank, just in case. I said maybe they'd only have sandwiches or a limited menu. I hadn't been impressed by the food since I had arrived, and felt that we would have a better choice in town than on the train.

We sat in one restaurant for a long time and finally asked if anyone spoke English.

"No."
"Do you have an English menu?"
"No."
"Could someone help us?"
"No!"

We left and found a friendly Chinese restaurant. The food was excellent. The service was good and the waitress actually smiled at us and thanked us for coming.

Back at the station, we grabbed our bags and boarded a train for Utrecht. At Utrecht, we hauled our bags down the steps, across the terminal, up the steps to another platform; all the while, asking for directions. No help was available. Noya was constantly warning me to watch my bag or someone would steal it.

At 9:45, the train arrived. We boarded and looked for our private, first-class compartment. The conductor grabbed our tickets, mumbled something and shoved us into our assigned compartment. It was not first class. And it definitely wasn't private. There were six bunks, with an Algerian man stretched out on the top one. He looked down at us and asked, "How far are you going?"

"Berlin," I said quietly.

Noya shot me a glance, not unlike my mother used to give me when I was a child and spoke to strangers.

"Speak any German?" he asked.

"No, neither of us does."

Noya glared at me.

He laughed. "Good luck. It's bad there for strangers. Especially women alone."

Now, I really needed that. I turned around, pulled the window down as far as it would go and took a deep breath.

"What are we going to do?" Noya asked, lighting a cigarette.

"We only have one tool here, let's try bribery," I said. "You try with the conductor. At least you're not an American. You'll do better."

She nodded and left the compartment. I returned my attention to the window and my deep breathing.

The Algerian spoke again, "If this is difficult for you, you could think of it as an adventure."

When someone says "adventure," it conjures up a mental picture of Indiana Jones, equipped with a whip, knife, gun and snakes in a situation with bad odds.

Back in Phoenix, when I had gotten cold feet just before taking the trip, an acquaintance, SueEllen, had said, "You'll have a wonderful time – it'll be a real adventure."

"What about the dining car? Where is it?" I asked.

"There is no dining car. There is no food available on this train." Our bunk mate found my question amusing.

Staring out into this strange land, I thought: What am I doing aboard a Polish train in a six-bunk compartment with an Algerian man and a Jewish friend with an Israeli passport heading for East Germany? Earl would definitely not approve. I wanted to cry.

Noya returned with the conductor. "Come," she said. We grabbed our bags.

"Good luck," said the Algerian.

"And to you," I smiled.

We were taken to another cushette compartment. It wasn't first class; but it would be private, the conductor promised. "Just keep the curtain drawn and the door locked," he said.

I wanted to be at home. I found it hard to believe I could be any more miserable than I had been at home, but I was.

The train moved east and we eventually were brave enough to change out of our jeans and into sweat clothes to sleep.

We made our bunks with a sheet and a blanket. I began to think that maybe I'd sleep – or at least try.

We stopped often. People got on, people got off. The train went forward, the train went backward. East German soldiers got on somewhere; and just as I was dozing off, someone tried to remove our door with incredible force.

"Open!" It was the military. We unlocked the door. A huge man (ten or twelve feet tall it seemed) pushed into our compartment and demanded our passports.

"Why is everyone so unfriendly?" I asked Noya.

"Don't be a child. This isn't a trip to Club Med. This is real. The soldiers are real. This is life in this part of the world."

I love Noya. She is so real.

"Are we crazy? Why in the hell are we doing this?" I wondered.

"As a Jew, I feel a need to visit East Berlin," she said.

"I feel a growing need to be sick," I said flatly.

We decided sleeping wasn't going to work, so we talked for hours. They were good hours – two friends sharing stories in the dark about the things most important to them. When the train stopped for two hours for some unknown reason, we hung out the window and talked to people on another train, stopped across the track from us.

"Where are you going?" I called out.

"To Poland," a young man replied.

"Do you have a tuna sandwich?" I asked.

Up until now, no one could speak or understand English. But for some reason, other people hanging out the window understood my question about the sandwich. It made everyone laugh.

We finally slept three or four hours before the military entourage came back to check passports again.

As I gazed out of the window through the heavy ground fog, the forest seemed to be full of unhappy war memories. I could hear the fear, the flights, the death. We could see barbed wire and military equipment all around us; plenty of evidence that this was not Des Moines.

By the time we arrived in Berlin the next morning, I felt much older and far less innocent than when my trip began. My personal grief over Earl's death seemed not as important as some of the larger issues in life.

As the train came to a halt, we gathered up our bags. My muscles were sore, making my bag feel even heavier than it did the night before. Our Chinese dinner had worn off hours before. We entered the terminal, searching for a restaurant. We spied one, went in, sat down and waited.

Any table where a man was seated got attention. We were ignored. Finally, Noya got up and brought back a waiter to take our order. No English menus – not much help. No potatoes, just pork and pancakes. We ordered two eggs and a roll.

I was tired. We arrived at the Penta Hotel and discovered that our room wouldn't be ready for many hours. We used the ladies room to freshen up and checked our bags with the bellman. We took a nine o'clock tour of West Berlin.

I found West Berlin to be a "lovely-to-look-at" town. Big trees and fine old buildings and churches. We were on the tour bus only minutes before we saw "The Wall." We got off. We were free; but just yards away, soldiers guarded the border and were prepared to shoot people who tried to leave.

Crosses with names and dates written on them were evidence of the reality of it all. I was uneasy.

After three hours, we grabbed lunch and hopped aboard another bus for our tour of East Berlin. Someone came aboard and warned us not to take pictures of anything or anyone military. No literature or books of any kind should be in view. Nothing could be taken from the bus. And money could not be changed for anyone who might ask us.

Our guide came aboard. She was a young woman in her twenties. She pointed out all the buildings and museums, told us how great the government was, how wonderful it was for young people and the many advantages of having a large family – such as reduction of interest and principal on mortgages. She said they earned about $1,000 a week and how wonderful it was there.

At the Russian Memorial, she told us about all the Russians who had died in service to their cause and their country.

I mentioned to Noya I found it interesting that no mention of any other soldiers was made and certainly no mention of the Jews who were killed. Something else very obvious was ignored, as well – The Wall – and it was everywhere.

Finally, I asked, "What about the wall?"

"The wall," she said, "is simply the border. It means nothing more."

While walking back to the bus, the young woman mentioned that she was very excited because she would be on holiday with her husband for the next few weeks.

"Gee, that's great," I said. "Are you going somewhere exciting or staying home?"

The words spilled from my mouth before I realized what I was saying. We both stopped and stared into each other's eyes. I was embarrassed. She couldn't speak. We just stood there looking at each other. A look passed between us that said it all.

"I'm sorry," I said at last. She smiled and nodded.

Back at the border, we sat for two hours while they all but stripped the bus. They inspected every niche and cranny and passed a long-handled mirror beneath the bus.

"Probably scared someone's trying to get in, since it's such a great place to live, don't you think, Noya?" I smirked.

It was good to be back on the west side again. Freedom felt good. But West German freedom was not good enough. I wanted to go home.

Suddenly, I was very grateful to be an American. I wanted to be with my children and with Earl. This was a difficult journey.

Chapter 16

*If you would indeed behold the spirit of death,
open your heart wide unto the body of life.
For Life and death are one, even as the river
and sea are one.*

Kahlil Gibran

Noya and I spent a couple of days in Berlin sightseeing, but mostly making observations. Seeing the Berlin Wall had been worthwhile. The time on the train, sharing our feelings and thoughts about life, getting to know each other better was the best part.

We still had the train ride back. At the station, we were once again faced with our communications problem. There were men at the station who worked there and spoke English. But they didn't want to offer any information.

We were tired of being treated poorly and were commiserating about the attitudes of the people, when a nice-looking couple approached us. The man gave us his card. He was a physician and told us that he was originally from India, but had lived in Berlin many years.

He said they had overheard our frustration, trying to secure information about our train. He apologized for the way we were being treated by his fellow countrymen. He then explained the Berliners' attitude was tied to their history and low self-esteem. He synopsized the people, their history and the way they'd been indoctrinated. He revealed as much about them as he did about his understanding and compassion for them — and us.

He and his wife kindly walked us to the correct platform, shook our hands, smiled and wished us a safe and pleasant journey. We thanked them. I took a deep breath, feeling much better. Noya once again cautioned me against letting go of my baggage.

"Someone will take it," she warned for the hundredth time.

"Noya, at this point, I'm hoping someone will," I said, wearily. "There's nothing of value in it except dirty clothes. And I'm tired of lugging them around."

The train coasted in and came to a stop. We boarded and found two seats across from a friendly couple. I had much to write about and got busy making notes. Noya and the couple visited. They were to become good and lasting friends.

The trip back was much better than the initial journey. When we reached Hanover, Noya and I parted company; saying our goodbyes until later in the week, when I would return to her home.

It was good to be with Leana, Friedy and their sweet little Kristina. Playing with Kristina took my mind off of myself and reminded me of how much I loved my own grandbabies. I looked forward to the one who would be arriving in May.

Leana and I took Kristina for long walks in the crisp cool air, enjoying the beautiful countryside with all the flowers and big trees. I wished Earl were there to share the experience. Home seemed so far away.

My stay in Germany was brief and I returned to Holland and the remainder of my stay with Terry and Noya. The days were endless and I became more and more restless.

After three weeks in Holland and Germany, I grew anxious to get to London. Terry was flying to Norway early on the morning I was leaving. Hitching a ride to the airport with him meant I had to get up at five a.m.

The ride to the airport with Terry was nostalgic. We reflected on our friendship – which had begun when they visited Earl and me soon after we married. We lived in Carmel then.

Later, we had visited with them in South Africa; then several times when they were in the States. And now, I was in Holland, without Earl.

Their friendship meant a great deal to me. And I was grateful to them for taking me in at this difficult time of my life. I saw Terry off, then poked around the shops and had tea to pass the several hours at the airport before my flight.

I was weary when I landed at Heathrow. I got a luggage cart and began to make my way through the crowd to customs. My cart had a wobbly wheel and fought me every step of the way. There were up ramps and down ramps. My arms ached from trying to control the cart with its heavy load.

Finally, I came to the maze before the customs counter. The line wound back and forth and finally I was abreast of the entrance to the agents. To the left of us was a row of six or eight seats.

A woman in uniform directed the line to go past the entrance, around the seats, making a full U to get back to where we already were standing. The space was narrow. I decided that since the line was moving quickly and my cart would slow everyone down, I'd wait for the men in front of me to go around the seats and come back to me before I moved ahead.

"You'll have to stay behind them," the women said to me.

"My cart has bad wheels and is hard to push, so I'm waiting here," I smiled.

"You must walk around the chairs," she commanded.

Well, flashes of the train, the German soldiers, the Berlin Wall and all the unfriendly people who wouldn't help us came to mind.

"I'm waiting here," I said flatly.

"You must move," she ordered.

"I'm not walking in circles for you or anyone else. There's no need for it. It accomplishes nothing," I said firmly.

"You will," she said angrily.

"No, I won't."

"Are you trying to upset our system?" she accused.

"Yeah, I sure am. Someone should."

At that point, the line had disappeared and it was my turn to go through the gate to the agent.

"You can't do that," she screamed.

"Watch me," I said.

I passed through the opening, up to the window and gave the agent my passport.

No one applauded, but I could feel Earl smiling. Wherever he was, he was smiling. He always hated it when the multitude played "follow the followers."

He always said, "Find out whatever the masses are doing and do the opposite and you'll probably never make another mistake again." Recalling that, I smiled all the way to the taxi.

I found the London taxis to be neat, clean and the drivers so courteous and civilized. Mine didn't speed, curse or otherwise endanger my life as others had in New York and San Francisco. The sun was out and the dry autumn leaves danced across the road and walkways as we made our way toward the little hotel.

It felt good to be free, to be with English-speaking, well-mannered people again. I took a deep breath and sat deeper into the seat. London was beautiful!

The hotel was quaint and comfortable. The concierge worried about me every day. He'd tell me if it was a good day to exchange money or not and gave me written directions on how to get to the train; which one to catch, where to get off and how to get home again. I had strict instructions to be sure and let the hotel know when I had returned safely home. I truly appreciated their concern.

One Sunday afternoon, I was resting in my room. I had a severe case of the Sunday blahs and an earache that later blossomed into a severe infection. I had rinsed out some personal items, listened to the soundtrack from *Phantom of the Opera* and was half asleep, lying on my bed.

It was late afternoon. I was on my right side, facing the wall with my eyes closed. But I became aware of a strange light and partially opened my eyes to see what it was.

On the wall, a bright pink pattern was forming with great intensity. Could it be the sun? How long had it been since I'd seen it. Ah, blessed sun! How I missed Arizona, its blue sky and sunshine.

I quickly rose, went to the window and peered out. Across the street and over a block, I could see the top of the magnificent Victoria and Albert Museum. The windows were bright neon pink-red, reflecting the setting sun. I reached for my camera.

Working quickly, I began shooting pictures of the rapidly changing scene before me. In a minute or two, it was over.

I put down my camera; recalling suddenly, my trip with Dan to the fishing camp in Alaska earlier that year, when Arte Wolfe was there.

Several of us had spent time taking pictures and gaining helpful tips from Arte as we visited the islands; taking pictures of plants, trees, scenes, bears, eagles, whales, otters and seals. Arte and the serious photographers carried tripods, investing long periods of time preparing, checking the light and setting their cameras at the correct speed.

I, on the other hand, was just interested in capturing the entire experience. I had my great Canon that does everything itself except jump out of the case and aim. I just saw great beauty I wanted to capture forever, aimed, shot and moved on.

Arte complained that I wasn't taking enough time to set up my shots. But we became friends in spite of my attitude. I kept wondering if the rest of them saw the big picture I did, and shared the complete experience that I'd had on those days. They spent so much time peering into their lenses and so little time seeing and enjoying all that was not in their view finder.

It reminded me of people who spend so much time preparing for life's experiences that the spontaneity goes out of it. Arte is an exception, I'm sure. Photography is his love and his living. And no one does it better. He immerses himself in the whole experience.

He savors every minute of preparation, anticipation. And he never misses a trick. His work must be very gratifying. His pictures are magnificent and breathtaking.

It was the others I was thinking about; and the experience I shared with them, compared with life in general. Sunsets and sunrises are such perfect examples. You can anticipate them for sure. You can prepare for them, yes. But once they begin, you must enjoy them and appreciate them at the moment, because they don't linger for you. They're here and gone. The sky quickly changes, the clouds take on colors of blue, pink, red and fade into a new night or a new dawn. Amazing! And, no two are alike. What splendor!

As I stood there, I remembered another time when Earl and I were in Florida on business. While there, we visited with friends on their boat. We left late in the afternoon from Port Charlotte to cruise to Sanibel and the South Seas Plantation for dinner. The weather was warm, the air was still and the water was as flat as a mirror. The sun was beginning to set in front of us, throwing reflections on the water that were so lovely, everyone had stopped talking to fully appreciate the spectacle.

I went below to get my camera to preserve the beauty for posterity. And as I came top side, I looked aft at the sky which already had become a very dark gray. Meanwhile, the moon had risen and was low, full and huge. It hung there like a moonshot from the *National Geographic Magazine.* I turned to tell everyone about the moon and saw that they were watching, in awe.

We all silently stared at the moon; then, almost on cue, we turned toward the sun now resting on the horizon in blazing shades of bright red and orange. The water was aflame, as our boat cut almost silently across the top of the mirrored reflection.

The air was soft on my skin and I felt suspended in a true twilight zone. It was unlike anything I had ever experienced. I couldn't speak. There was silence on board and all around us.

Soon the sun slipped from our sight and the moon rose as we veered toward the south; and, for the first time, we looked at each other, almost embarrassed.

Finally, someone spoke, "Was that something else, or what!?"

We spontaneously began to chatter excitedly. Each of us had been to a place and time that was never to be forgotten.

Through the years, Earl and I would remember the night we got caught between today, tonight, yesterday and tomorrow – "the twilight zone."

We saw our friend years later and the first thing he said was, "As long as I live, I'll never forget our experience that night on the boat."

Although sunsets are brief, memories of them and the people you share them with linger forever. Many times, when my children were small and we lived at the beach, families would get together after dinner on the beach to watch the sunset and wait expectantly for the "green flash," a natural atmospheric occurrence; quite spectacular, but rarely seen.

Seconds of greatness in life to be treasured – happy times, like the moon in South Africa.

I thought about the goals Earl and I always taught people to have. It's good to have goals and plans for our lives, and to know where we're going. But it's just as important to live our lives each and every day with an awareness and an appreciation of the unexpected, as life unfolds around us. We should grab every chance we get to participate in those moments.

Thank God, I've never been so sad or hurt or troubled that I couldn't lose the pain momentarily by watching a sunset or sunrise.

It's strange how it all works. It seems to me that right after Earl died, the severity of the pain I was experiencing increased my capacity to enjoy and appreciate the beauty of them even more.

I've watched shooting stars and meteor shows and

never once been distracted by my troubles. There's something bigger and more important than us going on out there; something grand and beautiful. And it's free for all of us to see and use and enjoy.

It doesn't matter where you're situated on the planet. The sun and moon and all the stars in the universe are visible to anyone who takes the time to look. Rich or poor, world famous or beggar – it's all the same. And the price is right. All you have to do is reach out and take it.

My thoughts continued to roam to another time, when Earl and I were in Orlando making a speech. We arrived at the airport to find they had overbooked and had given away our seats. Oh, sure, someone must have been sorry; although no one said they were. And it didn't seem to matter that we had to get to South Florida for another engagement.

Sure, we could complain to Eastern Airlines management; and we did. But no one really cared or made any concession for us. Left to solve our own problem, we finally chartered a small plane to get us there on time.

The rainy season in Florida is an amazing phenomenon. It can rain torrents for five minutes in one place, while half a mile down the road, it will remain dry.

We were in this tiny little plane shortly after takeoff, when we flew into heavy storm clouds. It was still daylight, so there was a beautiful, bright blue sky. Then, just over there, were big dark black clouds rimmed in reflections of the sun in gold and silver. Meanwhile, the lightning played ping-pong off the other clouds and there we were in the middle of it all.

It was exciting and exhilarating. There was so much to see, it was hard to keep up with the show. This went on for quite some time before we finally flew out of the rain and reached our destination.

Earl asked, "You weren't afraid were you, Honey?"

Weak in the knees, I replied, "Yes, I was, but I'd love to do it again."

He laughed and said, "That's my girl."

Earl and I used to play a game.

He'd ask, "Ever been to Chicago (or Greece or wherever)?"

And I'd say in a very serious voice, "Yes, of course, I've been *everywhere.*"

Then he'd say in an injured tone, "With – *him,* I suppose."

"Yes, with *the Earl,*" I'd say, with my nose in the air. "He took me *everywhere.* We did *everything.* He made all of my dreams come true!"

Earl would smile and give me a big hug. There was a silent sadness that went with the game; a knowing, somehow, that it would end too soon. And when it did, Earl wanted to know that he had taken me everywhere and left me with wonderful memories of our time together.

Here I was in England for the first time and without him. He had wanted so badly to take me to London.

"We'll go to Harrods. You'll love Harrods" – meaning he wanted to go again. Earl loved to shop. "And we'll sing, *If They Could See Me Now* when we get to Berkeley Square."

And so, the final days of my lonely flight to find my "journey into meaning" wound down.

I visited the usual sights of London and surrounding areas. I enjoyed Bath, a friend's lovely estate in Guildford, the theater and great English pubs. I went to Harrods for high tea and scones, then shopped. The trip was a whole lot cheaper than if Earl had been there with me. He would have bought out the place — one balloon at a time.

I joined other tourists at Buckingham Palace, where Earl had once been an invited guest. What a thrill it had been for him to visit the Palace and meet the Queen. The picture of Her Majesty receiving Earl hangs in our home. How he would have loved reliving it once again if he were here now, I thought.

While riding atop a sightseeing bus, I heard Earl's voice ask, "Ever been to London?"

The tears welled up in my eyes as I silently answered, "Yes, I've been everywhere ... with *him.*"

I could see him smiling.

When I visited Berkeley Square, I almost lost my courage. But then, very quietly, I began to sing the song we'd always planned to sing together, "If they could see me now, that old gang of mine... they'd never believe me, if my friends could see me now."

So, this Nightingale finally sang in Berkeley Square. I had learned much from my trip, including two very important things: one, that I hadn't gone far enough to outrun the grief and pain of losing Earl; and two, that I would probably survive it all somehow.

Chapter 17

*All deep things are song. It seems somehow the
very central essence of us, song;
as if all the rest were but wrappages and hulls.*
                              Thomas Carlyle (1840)

It was during my flight home from Europe that I gained a new perspective about my loss. I was looking out the window at the clouds, when I noticed a formation that looked like a bucking bronco.

I thought about my early years in Ohio and how my life path had led me to Florida, later California, and now Arizona where my environment was so different from anything I'd ever known before. It wasn't unusual to be sitting at a traffic light and see a person on horseback cross in front of the car.

I thought about the desert, the mountains. Then, all of a sudden, I had a flashback of the rodeo. The pictures in my mind played out a scene of a cowboy on a bucking bronco. And in a flash, there it was – my answer!

I'd been like that Bronco – wild, free and happy with Earl. And when he died, I had the full weight of the grief and loss thrown unexpectedly on my back. All these months, I had been trying to outrun my burden – bucking and kicking, screaming into the wind. But no matter how hard I tried, there it was.

Suddenly and clearly, I had my answer – this was my burden and like it or not, it was here to stay. My challenge now was to find a way to adjust to it, to carry it in such a way that I could go on with my life.

The realization that I could not escape my burden, but that I must accept it as part of me for the rest of my life, had a calming effect. I knew now why the handy dandy guide to overcoming grief hadn't made sense to me.

Even in my darkest hour, that little voice inside me was saying that I'd never get over it. Now, I knew I had to find a way around it; accept what had happened as a real and very important part of my life, my journey.

Returning home from Europe with this new realization that I would survive, I was now anxious to get on with my life. I now had the proof I was looking for. I'd been to "Des Moines" and returned with my prize. Having my answer and making it work, however, were completely different, as I was about to discover.

Tough times lay ahead, as I faced my first major holidays without Earl. I had celebrated my 50th birthday shortly after he died.

But now, Thanksgiving and Christmas were here. I put up a tree, trimmed it with all of our favorite ornaments, and did all the traditional things we had always done. But it hurt like hell. And the day after Christmas, I'd had all I could take. I walked into the living room, looked at the tree and told Dayne to "get rid of it."

I told myself all the positive things I would have told anyone else in my place. And I pushed through. But the tears flowed uncontrollably and the hurt and intense pain remained. I tried to become more stubborn in my war against my feelings of loss and abandonment.

By the end of December, I knew it was vitally important to my well being to at least try to find closure with Earl's death. Doing his work, giving speeches and keeping his ashes in the study was not a healthy way to get on with the business of living.

Just before New Year's Day, I decided it was long past time to scatter Earl's ashes. It was two o'clock in the morning. I sat at Earl's desk, holding the marble cube that contained what was left of him. The journey up the mountain would be difficult enough without carrying this heavy marble box. I sat there trying to figure out how to deal with this strange situation.

It occurred to me that people don't understand the

burden they place on their loved ones when they say, "Just scatter me somewhere on a mountain top." They don't think about how they'll get transferred or that maybe there will be some intense trauma to the loved one who has to carry their remains about.

This could not have been what Earl meant by keeping me "in a golden cage," protected from all pain. This was the real world.

Here, loved ones are left to settle estates, assume mountainous debts and scatter ashes.

The container had to go. My hands shook as I transferred the ashes to a Ziploc bag and put them in my fanny pack for the trip the next morning. I had gone to the nursery earlier that day and bought a package of poppy seeds to sow, along with the ashes, in memory of Earl and his love for California.

Sleep was difficult. Early the next morning, I put on my climbing gear and headed up a nearby mountain to perform my task of love and say goodbye at last to all that was left on earth of my husband.

The climb was difficult, both physically and emotionally. The slope was rocky, the ground sometimes loose. I kept losing my footing and sliding back.

Before long, I was hot, sweaty, tired, dirty, bruised and a little bloody from a fall. As I pushed on, I brushed past a cholla and was instantly stabbed by several cactus needles. I was amazed that they went right through my leather sneakers and two pair of socks.

I sat on a rock with tears streaming down my cheeks and removed the needles from my foot. Life had always been a challenge to me. And now, perhaps, I was experiencing the greatest one of all.

I knew I'd know the right place to scatter the ashes when I found it, and I did. It was beautiful there on top of that mountain. I could see forever in every direction. The wind blew through the brush while a pair of hawks flew over head, worried that I was there to disturb their nest.

I knew this was the right place and the right time.

Getting through New Year's Eve took all I had. I started the new year empty and numb. My commitment to adjust to my burden and accept my loss grew in intensity. I vowed regularly that I'd get through this and be in control of my life and my feelings once again.

I felt as if I were walking through a field of land mines. I'd wake up feeling good, sure of myself. And if someone asked how I was doing, I'd smile and say, "Really fine. I'm okay, now."

I'd get on with my day. And suddenly, unexpectedly, with the next step I took, my world would explode into tears. And all the feelings of loss and grief and missing would come flooding back.

There were times – sometimes hours, portions of a whole day – when I did not grieve. But even then, I hurt in that portion of my body where I felt Earl had been cut out of my physical world. It was in my heart, mostly, and in my stomach. Sometimes, it would build up in my chest and I'd have to fight hard to choke back the tears.

I was in such physical pain that if someone touched my arm, my skin burned. I felt like one big raw nerve. On the surface, for other people, I was remarkably able to laugh, maintain a positive attitude and make people believe that I had mastered my grief. But, it was there.

Earl died on March 25th, the day before Easter and exactly seven years to the fateful day I had flown to Carmel. The date was once again approaching. I'd have to find a way to make it through the anniversary of his death – somehow.

As the second week of March ended, I fought the need to scream in panic. I was reliving the previous year's events over again.

The phone was ringing, as I returned from the grocery store that Friday afternoon. It was my sister, Mary, calling to say that Mom, my other best friend, was dying. I'd better come quickly. I boarded the next plane to Ohio for another difficult flight in my journey.

Again, I would have to say goodbye to someone I

loved dearly.

It was very late when I arrived. My niece, Jackie, picked me up and took me to her house. She called the retirement home to see if we could come over. The supervisor said we could come in the side door and stay as long as we wanted.

Mother looked so small lying there in her bed. It was a month before her 92nd birthday. She had expressed her desire to go home to the Lord just a month earlier. She was in a deep sleep.

I carefully slipped up along side of Mom and lay down next to her. I put my arms around her and softly sang, *Go Tell Aunt Rhode*. Mother had always sung that to me when I was little and didn't feel well. Her breathing became more peaceful.

Toward morning, I went home with Jackie and slept for a few hours before returning with my sisters, Mary, Dorothy and Vanny. Our brother, John, was on his way from Florida.

Mother was still in her deep sleep. But sometimes, she would mumble something in a particular cadence that sounded familiar. After a while, I recognized it as the 23rd Psalm. I found Mother's Bible in her night stand and read it to her. From wherever she was, she would mumble the rhythm of the verses with me.

That evening, Mary and Dorothy took a short break and went home to get a bite to eat. It was late and Mother was tired. Each breath was an effort. I had been at the window earlier, looking at the spring buds on the trees that were trying to peek through the snow and ice.

I was talking with God and asked Him why He didn't let Mom come home. She obviously had done all she could here on Earth. She was old, tired and very ready. What possible value could there be in asking her to remain any longer?

Vanny and I were sitting next to the bed. I was holding Mother's hand. All at once, Mother began to smile. She opened her eyes, and was very present. She looked passed us and became absolutely radiant. She seemed to be looking at something that was beautiful and glorious.

We could not believe our eyes. Mother was experiencing something extraordinary that made her look strong, happy and ageless. She was beautiful! It was a look that neither of us had ever experienced. An incredible energy filled the room. Vanny and I were afraid Mother would feel she had to stay with us. So we let go of her hand and watched as she went happily and peacefully home.

I realized the answer to my question earlier when I asked God what purpose Mother could still have in lingering here. She still had one job to do. As a final act of love, God let Mother show us we do not die, but return ageless and beautiful to our Heavenly Father. She showed us the miracle of passing.

With Earl's and Mom's help, God was showing me a great deal about life and this thing we call death. I'd been so focused on my loss and my grief that I was missing the big picture.

Hadn't I criticized the photographers in Alaska for doing the same thing? Was that exercise in the hotel room in London the beginning of my awakening? I guess I had been learning more about my holiday on earth and my journey than I was able to see at that time.

I returned home after Mom's funeral. The next day, I had a business meeting in town. As I was drove home, a young woman turned in front of me at an intersection and smashed into my car. I sat there, badly shaken; the entire front end of my car wrecked and I thought, "This must be a test, to see how much I can handle."

Of course, the girl had no insurance.

Easter came and went. And in spite of my newly found insight, I cried most of the day and slept. My anniversary of grief was over.

I decided to work harder and be more in control of my feelings. To prevent ever getting hurt again, I'd guard against ever loving anyone again as much as I had loved and depended on my husband and my mother. And, by golly, it worked. Soon, I was once again in complete control of my life and feelings. In fact, I had managed to reach a point where I didn't feel anything at all. I was able to create a space for myself in which there would be no more tears, no more sorrow, no more pain – nepenthe.

Indeed, I had gotten around my grief. Trouble was, I had managed to rid myself of all the good feelings too. Life wasn't funny, or happy, or anything.

May came along; time for my yearly check up. I was lying on the examination table telling the doctor how well I was doing and how positive I was about my ability to get on with life.

Doctor Cohen looked down at me, a serious look on his face and said, "Diana, you have a lump in your breast."

The tears welled up and I felt sick to my stomach. "Well, I don't want a lump. Damn it! First, Earl died; then, Mom; then, an accident; and now, a lump.

"I don't want a lump," I repeated.

I thought, all those nights that I wanted to die after Earl's death and prayed so hard. What if the request just got to heaven? I should have remembered to cancel my order. I knew I didn't want to die.

"Not now, Lord, I decided to live, please," I pleaded.

The doctor arranged for me to go to the hospital the next day to have a mammogram and an ultrasound. The technician said she was optimistic about what she saw and wished me well. I picked up the films and took them to the surgeon.

As I waited to see the doctor, I was once again aware of how lost and alone I felt. I definitely was experiencing emotions again. How much more would I be asked to endure? What if it was malignant? What if I died? I didn't want to die.

The doctor came in and looked at the x-rays. He explained in a very friendly manner the best-to-worst-case scenario for me. He concluded in a very matter-of-fact way that if the lump were malignant, he'd just cut it out, along with my breast. And he'd just put a new breast in place of the old one. How simple he made it sound. He was even smiling.

I felt like I was falling through that black hole again. I fought for control and wondered, what if I have cancer and don't die and they "just cut it out." How did I feel about that?

I knew that I was more than a breast and wasn't less of a woman because I'd had my appendix or uterus removed. But, my breast – our society puts so much emphasis on a woman's breasts.

I thought of the many people I have known who have given up parts of themselves to cancer or accidents. And they are all wonderful people who keep on going, showing great courage and inspiration to those around them. They are productive and positive people whose respective "parts" were not the determining factor of their man or womanhood.

I knew that who I am and what I give to the world is determined by my attitude, my belief in myself. Still, I prayed, while the doctor prepared a needle with which to aspirate the fluid from my lump. "It'll just feel like a little bee sting," he said.

It didn't take long. But it was definitely more painful than a bee sting.

"We'll get the results and give you a call," he said as he walked out the door, leaving me alone on the table in the cold room.

Shaken, scared and sore, I drove myself home, poured myself a glass of wine and went out on the terrace. I watched the sunset. The breeze was warm, as I thought about my children and prayed that I would live.

I stayed outside for hours under the night sky. I thought about my life and what it meant to me. Earl's death seemed secondary now. It was as though someone had drawn me a big picture in perfect perspective.

My many blessings and reasons to live were too big to ignore and outweighed everything else. I had three wonderful children, who were big people now and my best friends.

When I was just a child myself, they were the thing I wanted most to have when I grew up. To double my blessings, they had given me grandchildren.

I had been Kim's coach when she gave birth to Danny, my first grandson. I'd helped bring him into this world that morning. And since, have been a major part of his life; and he, mine. Dear Sabra, my first granddaughter, was always wise beyond her years. She was just four years old when her daddy was killed on a motorcycle. It was she who brought perspective that day, after we found him.

Kim had been sedated and put to bed. Sabra was lying on the bed next to me in my room. She had been quiet for a long time; then looked up at me and asked, "Mimi, can we have sloppy-joes for supper tonight?" I guess I hadn't thought that far ahead. Of course we'd need to eat something.

"I don't have all the right ingredients to make sloppy-joes tonight, Honey. Maybe we can another night this week."

"How about pizza? That would make Mommy happy. She likes pizza."

"Pizza will be fine," I said, "But Mommy may not feel like eating. She's very, very sad."

"Why is she very, very sad?"

Sabra had been told that her daddy had died. Even though she was small, she knew something about the permanence of death – or I thought she did.

"Daddy was killed on a motorcycle today. He's not coming back and that's very, very sad."

"I know that!" she said. "Mommy told me. But, that's not very, very sad. It's only very sad." Then she went on to explain it to me.

"Sometimes when we watch TV, we see little children who live far away and they are very sick and don't have anything to eat. And their bones are sticking out. They cry all the time and have flies on their faces. They don't have beds and they are all dying. That's very, very sad.

"Daddy died and won't come back. But it's not as

sad as the kids on TV."

Sabra was young, too young to have gathered other people's attitudes about death. Her experience was limited. But boy, she was right on target.

She chose to wear her pink party dress to his funeral. She said it was her daddy's favorite.

And what about Jill and Jerome's new little boy, Jordan? He was just a couple of weeks old, and living right here in my house. Hadn't he been the center of my universe these past weeks? I had wrapped him in a blanket, taken him outside and showed him the moon for the first time when he was only days old. I wanted to be around to show him lots of other wonderful things, too.

I had too many good reasons to live. I couldn't die now. Besides my kids and grandchildren, I had my sisters and my brother. We had always loved each other and I had gained strength all my life knowing they were there for me.

I thought about all the running I had been doing to escape my pain; and again remembered the wild horses and how I had tried to get rid of the burden and the pain. Now, more than ever, I realized this unwanted weight was not really a burden, but a necessary new addition to the person I was becoming and meant to be.

I thought back to those first hours after Earl died, and his message about wearing scars with dignity. And I knew.

As I sat beneath the stars, I acknowledged out loud that people don't get over the loss of a loved one; that you never return to someone else's definition of normal and that things will never return to the way they were before the loss.

I acknowledged that life doesn't have to be bad or worse because of the loss. It just becomes different; and different can be good and wonderful and meaningful, if you just stop fighting and accept the events that occur on your journey.

I acknowledged that evening that no journey is without detours, disappointments and delays. But few of us would call off a trip because of any of these. The same must be true in life – we simply must keep on going, making the very best of each and every day while appreciating those who come into our lives to share our journey – even if they cannot be with us the whole way.

I realized that night that SueEllen and the Algerian on the train were correct. Life is an adventure. And I was right, too. Adventures are exciting, but not without confrontations with the devil himself. As Earl often said, "We may find ourselves in the vestibule to Erebus."

Indeed, but with courage, faith and the love of family and friends to support us, we can find our way back on the road to the rest of our journey. When we reach our final destination, we will have had many adventures and received many scars. But hopefully, we will have left behind something of value and perhaps something inspirational for others.

Each of us will experience loss and grief at least once in our lifetime. Some of us will repeat the experience many times. When we do, we feel that our loss is greater, more painful than the pain our fellow travelers experience. And to some degree, I believe that's true. Each of us bears his or her losses as deeply as he or she can feel them.

It's not for any of us to judge the degree to which someone else suffers; rather it is important to recognize the pain in other people's lives and to reach out and extend love to one another when someone needs it.

My painful detour has left me with scars that will remain a lifetime. But this experience, this acquaintance with death, has also deepened my relationship with God. I know now that dying is just part of the life cycle. And I know I want to live out the rest of my journey to its fullest.

Before all of this happened, my life was eventful – now it had become meaningful. I prayed that if God would let me stay a while longer, I would try to make my holiday on earth one of encouragement to others. I will focus on relieving pain in the world and rejoicing in my own pain, because it gave me insight to recognize the need in others.

My prayers did not go unanswered that night. There was no delayed answer. The lump was benign.

It was the turning point for me. I began my flight back to life with music. Since those early days of my childhood, when Mother and I sat at the piano in the evening and sang, music had been a constant companion. I like it all – classical, jazz, country, mood and rock n' roll.

I had found comfort listening to music during the months following Earl's death. Other times when I was having a bad day, *Send in the Clowns* used to play uncontrollably in my mind.

One of my favorite rock and roll songs is by Steve Winwood. He sings *Life's a Dance, Put on Your Dancing Shoes*, and that's exactly what I did.

At first, I thought dancing was such an unlikely thing to be doing at this time in my life. But after a few weeks of dance classes, I began feeling less stressful. I began to see my body take healthy shape, after more than a year of neglect. I slept well at night and I looked forward to going to the studio. It was the healthy exercise I needed.

Shortly after I started dancing, I picked up a copy of *Gifts from the Sea* by Anne Morrow Lindbergh and read, for the first time, her beautiful words comparing relationship to dance and I realized that dancing required trust and dependence on a partner. I needed to practice trusting again. This was my first step.

Slowly, the realization grew that our lives don't have to end when someone we love dies. What Earl and I had was wonderful and beautiful. And that didn't die. Earl didn't stop loving me and I didn't stop loving him. Our time together on earth simply came to an end. We shared a very special gift. The gift was love. It was hope. It was trust and it was time. Not a long time, but wide and deep; the things that dreams are made of.

The memory of those things and times are alive and well within me. I realize now that life doesn't always have to stay the same, to be good.

There are lots of different experiences, lots of expressions of life and a multitude of wonderful people out there waiting for us to come into their lives.

There was only one Earl Nightingale and only one relationship like ours. But Earl's death doesn't diminish the rest of my life and all of its possibilities.

On the final page of *Earl Nightingale's Greatest Discovery*, he wrote:

Being alive, just being alive, makes us winners. From then on, anything we want to add to the achievement is up to us. It needn't be a lot in the eyes of the world. But we can find our place in the scheme of things and do our thing – make our contribution, whatever it happens to be.

One morning recently, Diana and I were in Hawaii. It was five o'clock and still pitch dark, but the sky was clear and filled with stars. We put on our bathing suits and walked out into the water until it was up to our shoulders. We put our arms around each other and drank in the clean warm breeze and luxuriated in the sea, now warm to our bodies. And as we watched, the sky in the east grew softly lighter until the great, craggy old volcanic mountains were clearly outlined against the early morning sky. What a joy it was – what a joy it is – just to be alive!

I can imagine him saying, "Ever been to heaven?"

And, I'll answer, "Not yet. But when I get there, I'll see it... with Earl."

Epilogue

*I love thee with a love I seemed to lose
With my lost Saints, I love thee
With the breath,
Smiles, tears of all my life!
and, if God choose,
I shall but love thee better after death.*
                    Elizabeth Barrett Browning (1847)

One Saturday morning, about four weeks after Earl's death, I got up and wandered out to the kitchen to fix myself something to eat. I carried my breakfast over to our big, round kitchen table; and that morning, sat down in Earl's chair for comfort.

I took a bite of toast and gazed out through the windows at the mountainside, as we used to do every morning together.

And there —

caught up in a brittlebush,
was a bright yellow balloon
held fast by a blue ribbon,
as it danced in the morning sun.

Notes

Notes

Notes

Notes

Notes

Notes

Notes

Notes